VERY EASY
VEGETARIAN
COOKBOOK

NEW
HOLLAND

ALISON HOLST and SIMON HOLST – VERY EASY VEGETARIAN

First published in 1998 by New Holland Publishers (NZ) Ltd
Auckland • Sydney • London • Cape Town

218 Lake Road, Northcote, Auckland, New Zealand
14 Aquatic Drive, Frenchs Forest, NSW 2086, Australia
86 Edgware Road, London W2 2EA United Kingdom
80 McKenzie Street, Cape Town 8001, South Africa

Reprinted 1999, 2000 and 2001

Copyright © Text: Alison Holst and Simon Holst
Copyright © Photography: New Holland Publishers (NZ) Ltd

ISBN 1-877246-73-5

Food Styling: **Simon Holst** and **Alison Holst**

Home Economists: **Simon Holst, Alison Holst,
Jane Ritche** and **Sam Ford**

Props: **Jania Bates**

Editor: **Barbara Nielsen**

Designer/Production: **Sue Attwood**

Photographer: **Lindsay Keats** for all photographs
except for those on pages 16, 19, 20, 26, 38, 39, 43,
45, 65, 78, 90, 93, 101, 102, 112, 113 which are by **Sal Criscillo**

Printed through **Bookbuilders,** Hong Kong

Acknowledgements
Thanks to the following companies who provided food and products used in this book:
Alison's Choice for dried fruit, nuts, couscous, rice and bulgar,
Avocado Growers for avocados,
Eggs Incorporated for their support,
Bennick's Poultry Farm, Levin, for fresh eggs,
Bluebird Foods for **Empire** herbs and spices,
Ferndale and **Mainland** for parmesan, yoghurt and speciality cheeses,
Galaxy for blue cheeses,
Genoese Foods for pesto and tapenade,
Parex Industries for the **DeLonghi** contact grill,
Parkvale Mushrooms for gourmet brown mushrooms,
Sproutman Products for mesclun, fresh herbs and sprouts,
Tararua for grated cheese, cream cheese, cottage cheese and sour cream,
Unifoods for **John West** products,
William Aitken & Co Ltd for **Lupi** olive oil and balsamic vinegar.

Thanks to **The Lily House, Moore Wilson's,** and **Theme**, of Wellington,
and **The Garden Party** (Auckland) who provided the wonderful range
of tableware (see details below) used in the photographs.

The Lily House (Garden Party)
page 15 bowl and underliner, page 29 dip bowl, small bowl, square platter, page 31 dip bowls,
underliner and platter, page 37 blue red bowls, page 57 fork, page 58 serving plate,
page 61 plate and fork, page 62 bowls and plate, page 74 trug/basket and garden tools, page 81 plates,
page 82 plate, page 86 plate, page 89 plate and lizard, page 111 cups and plates, page 112 plate.
Moore Wilson's
page 23 bowl and underliner, page 24–25 platter and jars, page 33 red platter, page 40–41 platter,
page 57 small bowl, page 81 round board, page 94 oval platter, page 97 white bowls.
Theme
page 57 table mat, page 70 place mat, page 86 place mat, page 89 cutlery, page 112 jug.

VERY EASY VEGETARIAN COOKBOOK

ALISON HOLST
& SIMON HOLST

ABOUT THIS BOOK

We wrote our first vegetarian cookbook, *Meals Without Meat* about 10 years ago. At this time we were not really aware of the huge number of people who were interested in eating vegetarian meals, either a few nights a week, or full time.

A staggering 250,000 people have bought *Meals Without Meat*! We have received a great deal of feedback from cooks who swear by it, many of them telling us why they find it so useful. Simon's friends say they like it because it uses ingredients which they have on hand.

Alison is often told by women who cook for vegetarian children and meat-eating husbands that both groups like the food cooked from our recipes because it tastes great. This has surprised many meat-eaters who had previously considered vegetarian food bland.

As we have talked about vegetarian food in the last few years, many people have told us that, although they like the idea of vegetarian meals, they think these take a long time to prepare. We decided to write this book to prove that there are many interesting and tasty vegetarian recipes which are very easy. First, we had to decide how we should define this. Some people consider it means very simple or basic, and others feel that 'very easy' and 'quick' are more or less synonymous.

In the end, we decided to aim for simple but interesting recipes which can be prepared from start to finish in less than half an hour, (i.e. after work). There are always exceptions, however, and a few of our recipes, although quickly put together, take a little longer than 30 minutes to cook. We consider that these are easy too, as long as we can more or less forget about them while they cook.

Many younger cooks have told us that they want to make only one recipe for their main meal on most workdays. For this reason we have emphasised dishes which can stand alone, but we still offer extras for those occasions when they are required.

Don't worry if some of our ingredient lists look long! This doesn't mean that the recipes are complicated, but is often due to the seasonings we add to make a few simple, basic ingredients taste special.

ALISON HOLST AND SIMON HOLST

CONTENTS

VEGETARIAN KITCHEN

Meal preparation involves more than just cooking. Ingredients must be bought, too.
We hate shopping for dozens of ingredients at the end of a busy day, and suggest that, if you feel
the same way, you keep a stock of basic foods on hand, replacing what you have used, say, once each week.
This will quite often mean you can cook a meal without going shopping at all.

Here are some of the items that we keep on hand and use
regularly. Don't let the length of our list worry you – you don't need to buy everything at once!
You may already have some of them on hand, and the others can be purchased, a few at a time,
with your usual shopping.

USEFUL FOODS TO KEEP IN A CUPBOARD OR PANTRY:
long-grain rice (basmati has a lovely flavour; arborio or calrose
  rice are good for risottos)
pasta (preferably two or three different shapes)
Asian noodles
canned red kidney beans and chickpeas
canned tomatoes
canned corn
canned fruits (e.g. peaches, mangos, blueberries)
tomato paste
soy sauces (Kikkoman and dark)
vegetable stock powder or other stock
assorted dried herbs and spices
parmesan cheese
corn chips
potatoes, kumara* and onions
fresh garlic and ginger (for uncooked mixtures)

USEFUL FOODS TO KEEP IN THE FREEZER:
pastry (pre-rolled is a real bonus)
interesting breads (including flat breads)
flour tortillas
pre-grated cheddar cheese
frozen spinach
frozen peas

*sweet potato

USEFUL FOODS TO KEEP IN THE REFRIGERATOR:
eggs
an avocado (or two!)
mushrooms (buttons, cups or flats)
long-lasting vegetables (e.g. carrots, cabbage, celery)
one or two seasonal vegetables (e.g. zucchini, broccoli,
  red/green peppers, green beans)
fresh herbs
bean and/or other sprouts
salad greens (lettuce or mesclun)
salad dressing (homemade or bought)
lemons
apples
limes or bottled unsweetened lime juice
one or two types of pesto (e.g. basil and sun-dried tomato
  pesto)
bottled minced garlic
bottled minced ginger
bottled chopped coriander leaf
red or green curry paste
red chilli paste (bottled)
milk and yoghurt (lower-fat options)
cottage cheese, sour cream and cream cheese (lower-fat
  options if possible)
your favourite cheese
bread
filo pastry

Salads offer an easy and delicious way to eat more vegetables! Making an interesting salad from scratch can sometimes seem a real chore, but if you buy a prepared salad mix when you go shopping, you're three-quarters of the way there. Look for mesclun, for example. Good mesclun contains an interesting selection of baby leaf greens which look attractive and taste great. Pre-sliced coleslaw vegetables are also available, needing only the addition of homemade or bought dressing.

Look for living herbs which you can keep in water on the windowsill and use over a week or so, in salads as well as cooked food. Shoots and sprouts, too, provide interesting, nutrient-rich, tastes and textures all year round. Add one of our dressings (see pages 42-48) for a simple salad, or look in our salad recipes for new ideas and combinations.

Another of our favourite foods is the **avocado**. We are delighted that avocados are available nearly all year round. They may vary in variety, with differing colour, shape, size and skin texture but, whatever their appearance, you can tell whether they are ready to eat by seeing if they 'give' when pressed gently at the stem end. (Do this rather than squeezing them.) Half an avocado makes an 'instant' lunch with only 150 calories (the equivalent of half a packet of 2 minute noodles) and will stop you feeling hungry all afternoon! As well as tasting great and requiring little or no preparation, avocados are a good source of folate, potassium, Vitamin E and fibre. They contain no cholesterol, are rich in mono-unsaturated oil (the 'good' oil in olives and olive oil) and have been approved (given the tick!) by the Heart Foundation.

You can now buy many partly prepared products that can make a cook's life much simpler. Individually they may seem like small things, but each means that you add flavour and character to your cooking with savings of time, hassle and mess! These are products like bottled minced garlic and ginger ,which are wonderfully convenient in recipes in which they will be cooked. We have referred to bottled minced red chilli many times throughout this book. It is easily measured and provides consistent heat and flavour. Bottled coriander is the best substitute for the real thing that we have found, and we use it happily when we do not have fresh coriander leaf on hand. We have used the **John West brand** wherever bottled flavourings are called for in this book.

After some thought, we decided to use **food processors** in some recipes, since they purée many foods so efficiently and make a cook's work so much faster and easier. If you don't have one, look around! After making sure that none of your relations have one which they no longer use, check out some of the smaller, inexpensive machines which have appeared in the past few years. (A friend of ours recently bought a small processor very cheaply.) If you can't find something to suit your purse, buy a second-hand mouli, rather than bypassing our puréed soups!

If you like the flavour and texture of roast or grilled vegetables and want to prepare these easily, in a short time, check out De Longhi's double-sided electric grill, called a **Contact Health Grill**. It leaves attractive grill marks on a variety of vegetables and cooks evenly and quickly, with only a little added oil. We have used these excellent machines for the past year and have found them especially good for thickly sliced eggplant, roasted mushrooms (particularly flats), and quartered red and yellow peppers. (During the last minute of cooking, we often brush our vegetables with a little pesto mixed with olive oil, for even more delicious results.)

Using **pre-grated cheese** saves time and grated knuckles. Store it in the refrigerator for a few days, or use it straight from the freezer, where it may be kept for months. Pre-rolled pastry and filo are two useful products, which in our opinion put piemaking into the 'very easy' category.

Canned beans are another excellent product to keep on hand when you want a meal on the table quickly! Sadly we don't have the range of canned beans available in the US, UK and Europe, but we were very pleasantly surprised by the variety of different and delicious dishes we could make with canned red kidney beans and chickpeas.

When we wrote *Meals Without Meat* only button mushrooms were available year round. We now have a variety of **mushrooms** to cook with, and enjoy them often, considering brown 'stuffing caps' and 'flats' excellent for 'very easy vegetarian' meals. We find them particularly popular with 'part-time' vegetarians, because of their dark colour, chewy texture and definite flavour. If you have been unsure how to use brown mushrooms, we hope our recipes will inspire you!

Ten years ago **pesto** was used only by the few people who made their own. Now that top quality commercially made pesto is readily available, we recommend it as a useful and versatile product to keep on hand. We love it and regularly use it as a seasoning when cooking, and in other ways as well. Try it mixed with oil and brushed on bread before grilling to make delicious crostini (see page 22), or serve it as a dip with vegetable crudités. A platter of bread, crackers, cheese and different types of pesto makes a great snack or starter. For a simple meal, stir your favourite pesto through cooked pasta, or mix it with cottage cheese, sour cream or cream cheese for an instant topping, sauce or dip, or a quick and tasty filling for a baked potato or kumara (sweet potato).

Bread is an important food. A good loaf of bread turns an ordinary meal into something substantial. Better still, bread is good for you! Low in fat, high in complex carbohydrates and fibre (especially wholemeal bread) it is a food which we can eat as a filler, without guilt! A wide range of interesting breads is available from in-store and specialty bakeries. Keep a selection on hand in your freezer, or invest in a bread machine and enjoy your own warm, homemade bread.

Eggs – Convenience Plus!

What could be faster, easier and more satisfying than an egg? Conveniently packaged within each shell is some of the highest-quality protein available, along with an impressive assortment of vitamins and minerals. Eggs deserve recognition for being one of the most reasonably priced, healthful and nutritious convenience foods available!

Great on their own or incorporated in other dishes – you'll find them used throughout our book!

Those cooking for vegetarians should be aware that some foods contain 'hidden' animal products. These do not concern everybody, but are important to some. Many cheeses for example, are made with animal rennet – look for the growing number of vegetarian rennet cheeses if this is a concern. Avoid products containing gelatin and check that the vegetable stock you buy does not contain animal fats. Some Thai-style curry pastes contain shrimp paste, and fish sauce is out for obvious reasons. In short read labels very carefully.

EATING WELL

As well as tasting and looking good, the food you eat should be good for you,
keeping you healthy, strong, and in peak condition.

It is really important to eat a good variety of foods. A wide range of foods in your diet keeps it
interesting and well balanced, as nutrients that one food lacks are supplied by others.

Although you do not need to know the details of all the foods you eat, knowing a little about the four
main food groups, and choosing foods from each group, each day, will ensure your diet is well balanced.

FRUIT AND VEGETABLES
Make sure you have five servings (or more!) each day. Eat salads, cooked and canned vegetables, vegetable-based main courses, and canned fruit. Fresh fruit and dried fruit make good snacks.

BREADS AND GRAINS
Each day, eat at least six servings of grain-based foods such as bread (1 slice is 1 serving), breakfast cereal, pasta, rice, couscous, and kibbled grains. (Include some whole-grain products.)

MILK AND DAIRY PRODUCTS
Select at least two servings a day. Look for reduced-fat milk, yoghurt, cottage cheese, cheese, etc. (Vegans can replace milk with soy milk fortified with calcium and Vitamin B12.)

EGGS, NUTS, SEEDS AND DRIED BEANS, PEAS AND LENTILS
Choose at least one serving a day from this group. (Choose recipes from different sections of our 'Main Events' through the week*. Nuts and seeds make good snacks. (Non-vegetarians include meat, fish and poultry in this group, too.)

When you plan your daily food, remember that it is important not to eat too much fat, sugar and salt.

Keep a healthy weight with regular exercise as well as healthy eating.

*Until relatively recently vegetarians were told about the importance of protein complementation. This was a system in which different plant proteins were combined in a single meal in order to give a complete set of the essential amino acids (protein building blocks). More recent nutrition research has shown that a varied vegetarian diet provides sufficient complementary proteins during the course of one or several days.

VERY EASY VEGETARIAN
SATISFYING SOUPS

When the weather is cold and wintry and you want a quick meal to 'warm the cockles of your heart' and make you feel that the world is a better place, serve a bowl of homemade, warming soup!

Try some of our soups from the following pages; some are new and some are old favourites, modified so they are suitable for vegetarians. We have also streamlined a number of recipes to make them easier, so that none of them take longer than half an hour to prepare.

None of the creamy soups call for white sauce – they are thickened by puréed (or mashed) vegetables and simply have cream cheese, sour cream, fresh cream or evaporated milk stirred in. Similarly, none call for dried beans, which take hours to cook – instead we have opened a can or used red lentils which boil up tender in only 15 minutes.

If you like the idea of cooking once for two or three meals, make plenty! As long as you refrigerate it promptly, your soup will keep for several days, and the flavour will often actually improve during this time.

These soups are all substantial enough to serve as the main part of a meal, especially when accompanied with your favourite bread, plain, toasted or heated in the oven. We love the contrasting textures of crusty bread and smooth, thick soup, and feel they are perfect partners.

When you want your soups to look and taste extra-special, let your friends add a variety of crunchy, creamy and fresh-tasting toppings. You may think this sounds strange but we are sure that after you try them once, you will be hooked on the idea!

Last but not least, if you are trying to get the 'eat more vegetables' message across, your soup pot will be your ally! Many reluctant vegetable eaters will hold out their bowl for more soup, without realising just what is in it! We think soup is one of the nicest things about cold weather – try our recipes and see if you agree.

Thai Pumpkin Soup

PASTA AND BEAN SOUP

This delicious soup is substantial enough to serve as a complete meal, but may be made in 15–20 minutes, since it contains canned rather than dried beans.

FOR 5–6 LARGE SERVINGS:

1 large clove garlic
1 medium–large onion
2 tablespoons olive oil
2 small dried chillies or ½ teaspoon minced red chilli
2 bay leaves
¼ teaspoon dried thyme
425g can Italian seasoned tomatoes
425g can red kidney beans
440g can four bean mix
4 cups vegetable stock or 4 teaspoons stock powder
   and 4 cups water
1 cup small macaroni or other small pasta
about 1 teaspoon salt
black pepper to taste
basil pesto (or parsley) and parmesan cheese

Finely chop the garlic and onion. Heat the oil in a large pot, then add the garlic and onion and cook without browning until the onion is soft and clear. Stir in the crushed chillies, whole bay leaves and thyme and cook for a minute longer.

Add the contents of the cans of tomatoes and beans, then the stock. Bring to the boil then add the pasta. Simmer, stirring occasionally, until the pasta is tender (10–15 minutes) then taste and add salt and pepper.

Top each serving with a teaspoonful of basil pesto (or chopped fresh parsley) and freshly shaved or grated parmesan cheese.

MAKING HOMEMADE STOCK:

To make quick homemade stock, grate coarsely or chop finely in a food processor 1 large carrot, 1 large onion and 2 or 3 stalks of celery. Crush and add 1 teaspoon of minced garlic and ½ teaspoon of minced chilli. Simmer mixture in a large pot with 6 cups of water for 20 minutes, adding some dried herbs and pepper as vegetables cook. Strain, squeeze as much liquid as possible from the solids, then add a teaspoon each of salt and sugar. Use or freeze.

THAI PUMPKIN SOUP

The colour, interesting flavour and 'velvet smooth' texture make this a wonderful soup to serve to guests.

FOR ABOUT 8 LARGE SERVINGS:

2 medium-sized onions
2 tablespoons olive oil
2 teaspoons green curry paste*
4 cups vegetable stock or 4 teaspoons stock powder
   and 4 cups water
2 medium-sized carrots
1kg peeled and seeded pumpkin
2 medium-sized kumara
400ml can coconut cream
1 tablespoon Kikkoman soy sauce
fresh coriander leaves

Finely chop the onions, then heat the oil in a large pot. Add the onion and cook until it is transparent but not browned.

Add the curry paste (which is bought in a jar or foil packet) and cook for 2–3 minutes longer, stirring often, before adding the stock or water and stock powder.

Slice the carrots thinly (5mm thick) and add to the pot so they start cooking while you cut the pumpkin and kumara into 1cm cubes, then add them too. Cover and cook for 10–12 minutes or until the vegetables are tender. (For best flavour and colour, do not cook longer than necessary.)

Blend or food process in batches, then pour through a sieve back into a clean pot. Add the coconut cream and soy sauce, and bring back to the boil. Adjust seasonings if necessary.

Serve immediately or reheat when required, garnishing each serving with a sprig of fresh coriander, or with finely chopped coriander leaves.

* See pages 8–9.

VARIATION: Semi-vegetarians and non-vegetarians may like to replace the soy sauce with 2 tablespoons fish sauce.

FROZEN HOMEMADE STOCK:

Keep homemade vegetarian stock in lidded plastic tubs and cartons (or plastic milk or cream bottles) in the freezer. Don't fill containers right to the top since stock expands during freezing. One cup quantities are particularly useful since they thaw fast in the microwave or in your soup pot.

Pasta and Bean Soup

BROCCOLI AND BLUE CHEESE SOUP

This version of an interesting and popular soup suits the theme of this book. If you like, replace the blue cheese with a few tablespoons of grated parmesan cheese to give the soup a different but equally delicious flavour.

FOR 4 LARGE SERVINGS:

1 large onion
2 tablespoons olive oil or butter
1 teaspoon (1–2 cloves) minced garlic
2 medium-sized to large potatoes (about 400g)
2 cups vegetable stock or 2 teaspoons vegetable stock
    powder and 2 cups water
500g head of broccoli
$1/4$–$1/2$ cup cream cheese
$1/2$ cup milk
blue cheese to taste, up to 50g ($1/2$ wedge)
extra milk ($1/2$–1 cup)
salt to taste (probably about $1/2$ teaspoon)
freshly ground black pepper to taste
1–2 tablespoons basil pesto, optional

Peel and finely chop the onion then heat the oil or butter in a fairly large pot. Add the onion and garlic and stir to mix. Cook gently with the lid on, without browning, while you scrub the potatoes, then cut them into 1cm cubes.

Add the potato cubes and the stock (or stock powder and water), cover again and simmer until the potatoes are tender, about 10 minutes.

While the potatoes are cooking, chop the heads off the broccoli, cut them into pieces the size of small marbles, then peel the stalks, starting at the bottom. Chop the peeled stems into 5mm lengths. Add the prepared broccoli to the potato mixture, cover and cook for 5–10 minutes longer, until the broccoli is tender but still bright green.

Purée this mixture in a food processor. Add the amount of cream cheese you like (the larger amount makes it richer) then add the first measure of milk. Add the blue cheese in teaspoon-sized lots, processing and tasting after each addition, until the soup has the strength of flavour that suits you. Add extra milk until it is the thickness you like, then adjust seasoning to taste, with salt, pepper, and pesto for extra flavour if desired.

Refrigerate if soup is not to be reheated and served immediately. Serve topped with a swirl of cream, sour cream, or cream cheese thinned with milk.

CHUNKY CORN CHOWDER

A large can of creamed corn added to a few basic finely chopped vegetables will make a substantial soup with an interesting texture and flavour in a short time.

FOR 4–5 LARGE SERVINGS:

2 large onions
1 cup finely chopped celery, optional
2 tablespoons butter or olive oil
2 medium-sized scrubbed potatoes
$1^1/2$ cups vegetable stock or $1^1/2$ teaspoons green herbs
    stock powder and $1^1/2$ cups water
410g can creamed corn
$1/2$ cup water
1 cup milk
$1/2$ cup sour cream, cream, cream cheese or evaporated milk
1 tablespoon basil pesto, optional
$1/2$ teaspoon or more salt
pepper and Tabasco sauce to taste

Chop the onions and celery (if available) into small (about 5mm) cubes. Cook over moderate heat in a medium-sized pot in the butter or oil (or a mixture), without browning, while you prepare the potatoes.

Cut the unpeeled potatoes into 5mm slices, then into 5 mm cubes. Add them, all at once, to the onions, add the stock then cover and simmer over moderate heat for 4–5 minutes, until potato is tender.

Add the creamed corn, rinse out the can with the water and add it, the milk, the sour cream, cream, cream cheese or evaporated (unsweetened condensed) milk. Stir or whisk everything together. Bring to the boil, simmer for about a minute, then take off the heat and stir in the pesto. Season to taste with the salt, pepper and Tabasco.

Reheat when required, without prolonged boiling, adding some chopped parsley, fresh herbs or thinly sliced spring onion leaves if any of these are available. Serve with buttered toast or warmed crusty rolls.

EXTRA OPTIONS: Half a red or orange pepper, chopped as finely as the onions, and added to the oil before the potatoes, gives the chowder extra flavour and colour. A few green beans or some broccoli, chopped finely and added at the same stage, are good too.

Chunky Corn Chowder

BROWN MUSHROOM SOUP

Make this chunky, robust soup from mature 'wild' field mushrooms, or, more realistically, from big flat brown mushrooms gathered from your nearest supermarket!

FOR 4 LARGE SERVINGS:

2 medium-sized onions
3 tablespoons butter
1 teaspoon (1–2 cloves) minced garlic
4–5 large flat brown mushrooms
$1/4$ teaspoon dried thyme
3 tablespoons flour
2 cups vegetable stock or 2 teaspoons stock powder
   and 2 cups water
$1/2$ teaspoon salt
pepper to taste
1 tablespoon sherry, optional
1 tablespoon wine vinegar or balsamic vinegar
2 cups milk

Peel and finely chop the onions. Melt the butter in a large pot, add the onions and cook over a medium heat for about 5 minutes until the onions are evenly browned, then add the garlic and cook for 1–2 minutes longer. Chop the (cleaned) mushrooms finely and add to the onions with the thyme. Cook for 5 minutes, stirring often.

Stir in the flour, cook until it has lightly browned too, then add the stock (or stock powder and water), salt and pepper, sherry and vinegar. Stir well to mix, bring to the boil, then simmer for 5–10 minutes.

Stir in the milk, heat until almost boiling, then serve with sliced rolls, which have been buttered or brushed with oil (and pesto if you like) then grilled until lightly browned.

PESTO SOUP TOPPER:

Pesto livens up any soup which seems a little bland. After adjusting its seasoning, stir a tablespoon of your favourite pesto into the soup before it is served, or thin pesto with a little olive oil and let everybody add a teaspoonful to their own soup bowl, OR stir pesto into sour cream and drop a spoonful on each serving, swirling it attractively.

SPINACH SOUP

As long as you do not overcook it, this soup has a wonderful bright green colour. A little cream 'softens' the flavour and makes it popular with many people who do not enjoy plainly cooked spinach.

FOR 4 LARGE SERVINGS:

1 large onion
1 tablespoon butter
$1/2$ teaspoon freshly grated nutmeg, if available
2 large potatoes
3 cups vegetable stock or 3 teaspoons stock powder
   and 3 cups water
250g spinach
$1/2$ cup cream
$1/2$ cup milk
salt and pepper

Chop the onion finely and add to the melted butter in a fairly large pot. Add the nutmeg, cover and cook gently for 5–10 minutes, without browning.

Scrub the potatoes and cut into 1cm cubes. Add to the pot with the stock or stock powder and water.

Cover and bring to the boil, then simmer for about 15 minutes, or until the potatoes are tender. Add the well-washed, roughly chopped spinach and simmer for 3–4 minutes longer, until the spinach is tender but still bright green.

Purée everything in a food processor, blender or mouli, in several batches if necessary, then pour back into the pot. Whisk in the cream and milk, adding more milk if you want it thinner.

Taste, and adjust the seasoning if necessary, adding extra salt, freshly ground pepper and nutmeg.

Reheat briefly just before serving plain, with a swirl of plain or lightly whipped cream, or with croutons, or Melba toast.

NOTES: Chop the greens finely and mash the soup instead of puréeing it, if you don't have a suitable machine. If you like, use young silver beet leaves instead of spinach. The flavour is good but milder and different, and the colour is not as bright.

Keep vegetarian stock on hand. Look in a large supermarket to see what commercially made stocks are available. Check tetrapack, canned and plastic bagged stocks as well as instant stocks, reading labels carefully to check that they contain no unwanted ingredients.

Brown Mushroom Soup

QUICK TOMATO SOUP

If you have found the perfect ready-made tomato soup at a reasonable price, you won't need this recipe. If you haven't, try our 7 minute version, which we think is well worth the little effort involved!

FOR 4 LARGE SERVINGS:

1 tablespoon olive or other oil
1 teaspoon (1–2 cloves) minced garlic
1 teaspoon ground cumin or curry powder
2 tablespoons flour
425g can tomato purée made up to 4 cups with hot water
grated rind ½ lemon, optional
1½ teaspoons sugar
250g carton (1 cup) sour cream
salt and Tabasco sauce to taste
1–2 tablespoons basil pesto

Heat the oil in a medium-sized pot. Add the garlic, and cumin or curry powder and the flour and stir until bubbling.

Stir in about a cup of the purée and water mixture, then bring to the boil, stirring all the time. Add the remaining tomato mixture with the grated lemon rind and sugar, and bring to the boil.

Whisk, or beat in the sour cream with a fork, remove from the heat and season to taste. Add 1 tablespoon of basil pesto, taste, and add more if you want a stronger herb flavour.

Just before serving, reheat, without boiling.

Serve with buttered toast, toasted cheese sandwiches, warmed bread rolls, or sliced French bread, which has been lightly buttered or oiled, and browned under a grill.

EXTRA OPTIONS: Top each serving with a little plain, unsweetened yoghurt and a sprinkling of fresh herbs, thinly sliced spring onions or finely diced avocado tossed in lemon juice to delay browning.

GREEN SALSA SOUP TOPPER:
Gently stir together 5mm cubes of ripe avocado with a little lemon or lime juice and finely chopped spring onions. Add fresh or bottled coriander leaves and finely chopped pickled Jalapeno peppers if you have them. Allow 1–2 tablespoons for each serving.

KUMARA, PUMPKIN AND PEANUT SOUP

This combination makes a popular and interesting soup with a complex flavour. Alison has been thanked by several restaurateurs for this recipe.

FOR 4 LARGE SERVINGS:

1 large onion
2 tablespoons butter or oil
1 teaspoon (1–2 cloves) minced garlic
½ teaspoon curry powder
½ teaspoon ground coriander, optional
⅛–¼ teaspoon minced red chilli
1 fairly large (250g) kumara
250g–350g pumpkin
4 cups vegetable stock or 4 teaspoons stock powder
   in 4 cups water
½ teaspoon salt
2 tablespoons peanut butter

Finely chop the onion. Melt the butter (or heat the oil) in a medium-sized pot. Add the onion and garlic and cook over low heat, without browning, until the onion is transparent. Add the curry powder, coriander if you have it, and minced red chilli (as much as you like for hotness) to the onion mixture and stir over moderate heat for about a minute longer.

Chop the prepared kumara and pumpkin into 1cm cubes. (Use more pumpkin if you like, but do not use extra kumara or the soup will be too sweet.) Add the vegetables to the pot, add the stock or stock powder and water, bring to the boil and simmer for about 15 minutes or until the vegetables are tender. Add the salt then the (smooth or crunchy) peanut butter. (Too much peanut butter will overpower the vegetables.)

Purée in a food processor, blender or mouli (or for a soup with some texture, crush with a potato masher). Adjust the seasoning to suit your taste, and reheat.

Serve topped with yoghurt or coconut cream, finely chopped roasted peanuts and chopped coriander leaves.

EXTRA OPTIONS: Use less stock or water and thin the soup down with coconut cream.

Pile goodies on top of thick soup, especially if it is the main part of your meal. Contrasting textures and colours are best. A handful of small croutons, with an interesting raw vegetable salsa and a spoonful of yoghurt or sour cream turn any soup into something special.

Kumara, Pumpkin and Peanut Soup

WHITE GAZPACHO WITH GRAPES

This cold soup makes a great dinner party starter or a lightish main meal on a hot summer's evening. Even though it sounds rather strange, we think you should try it, especially if you like tomato-based gazpacho.

FOR 6 STARTER OR 4 LARGE SERVINGS:

4 slices stale (firm-textured) white bread
2 cloves garlic
1$\frac{1}{2}$ teaspoons salt
1 cup (100g) ground almonds
$\frac{1}{2}$ cup olive oil
$\frac{1}{4}$ cup white wine vinegar
4 cups iced water
40–50 green seedless grapes
12 ice-blocks
croutons

Choose bread with some body and character if possible. Cut off its crusts then soften by pouring some cold water over it. Leave to stand for a minute or so, then squeeze out (and discard) most of the liquid, then put the bread in a food processor with the peeled garlic cloves, salt and ground almonds. Process to a smooth, thick paste. (The garlic gets chopped more efficiently in a thick mixture.)

With the motor running, pour in the oil in a thin stream, as if making mayonnaise. Add the vinegar, then add one cup of the iced water.

Tip into a large bowl or jug, then stir in the remaining 3 cups of water. Chill for up to 24 hours, tasting and seasoning just before serving.

Serve the soup very cold. Drop about 8 halved grapes and one or two iceblocks into each serving, then let your friends and/or family help themselves to lots of crisp, freshly made, small croutons.

RED LENTIL, CARROT AND KUMARA SOUP

Red lentils cook fast, without soaking, so you can make this tasty and substantial soup in about half an hour. We are sorry that the ingredient list looks long, but it's the flavourings that make it taste so good.

FOR 4 LARGE SERVINGS:

1 large onion
2 tablespoons olive oil or butter
1 teaspoon (1–2 cloves) minced garlic
$\frac{1}{4}$–$\frac{1}{2}$ teaspoon minced red chilli
2 teaspoons ground cumin
1 teaspoon turmeric, optional
4 cups vegetable stock or 4 teaspoons stock powder
    in 4 cups water
$\frac{3}{4}$–1 cup red lentils
2 medium-sized carrots
2 stalks celery
1 large kumara
$\frac{1}{4}$–$\frac{1}{2}$ cup cream, optional
salt and freshly ground black pepper
basil pesto

Chop the onion in 1cm chunks and cook in the oil or butter for about 5 minutes, without browning. During this time, stir in the next four ingredients. The spices should smell fragrant, but should not burn.

Add the liquid and the lentils (more makes a thicker soup), and simmer, stirring now and then, while you cut the carrots and celery in 5mm slices, and the thinly peeled kumara in 1cm cubes. Add them and cook gently, with the lid tilted, for 15–20 minutes, or until everything is tender.

Leave the soup chunky, or purée all or part of it, depending on the texture you like. Thin with extra stock, water or milk if very thick. Add cream or sour cream if you like. Taste and season last of all.

To serve, top with spoonfuls of basil (or other) pesto.

EXTRA OPTIONS: A few minutes before serving, stir into the soup small cubes of tofu. Sprinkle parmesan on individual servings. Replace kumara with potatoes.

FOR VEGANS: Make with oil and without milk or cream.

White Gazpacho with Grapes

CREAMY GREEN PEA SOUP

With peas from the freezer and a carton of cream cheese, you can make a bright green, tasty, substantial and filling soup.

FOR 3–4 LARGE SERVINGS:

1 teaspoon (1–2 cloves) minced garlic
1 tablespoon olive oil or butter
4 cups free-flow frozen peas
1 cup water
250g carton cream cheese (low fat or regular)
1 teaspoon herb-flavoured salt or stock powder
1–2 cups milk
seasonings to taste

Heat the garlic in the oil or butter until bubbling but not brown, then add the frozen peas and water, cover and cook for 4–5 minutes until peas are tender but still bright green.

Purée in a food processor with the herb-flavoured salt or stock powder and (previously stirred) cream cheese. Thin with 1–2 cups of milk to reach the thickness you like.

Adjust seasoning, adding salt, pepper and Tabasco to taste. Sieve part or all of the soup if you want it smoother, or eat without sieving.

Refrigerate for up to 2 days, thinning with water or milk as necessary.

Serve with warmed, crusty, crunchy bread.

Top each serving with spoonfuls of sour cream and basil pesto, or with tiny croutons, sour cream and tomato salsa.

EXTRA OPTIONS: If you have them, cook several chopped lettuce leaves and/or spring onions, and a dozen or so fresh mint leaves with the peas.

TOMATO SALSA SOUP TOPPER:
Stir together 5mm cubes of really red (preferably oval Italian) tomatoes, and red onion or thinly chopped spring onion, and add small cubes of unpeeled cucumber and chopped fresh basil leaves or coriander leaves if available. Add a dash of balsamic or wine vinegar, and a little salt and sugar. Allow 1–2 tablespoons per serving.

CRUNCHY BREADS TO SERVE WITH SOUP

Interesting, crunchy breads with soup make a satisfying meal. If you can buy firm-textured crusty bread, you may not want to read any further. If you can't, use some of the following ideas to firm up and add interest to softer breads, and/or to revitalise stale bread.

CROUTONS

Cut toast thickness bread into very small cubes (using a sharp serrated knife) and put these in a large bowl. Measure into any small container a tablespoon of olive oil for each thick slice of bread you cut up. Drizzle the oil into the bowl of bread while you toss it lightly with a fork or your other hand. Leave as is, or sprinkle lightly with herb, garlic or onion salt, your favourite seasoning mix or a little curry powder, paprika, etc.

Heat in a frying pan over low heat, turning at intervals, for about 20 minutes or until golden brown, OR spread on a large shallow dish and bake in a preheated oven at 150C° until golden brown, about 5 minutes, OR brown under a moderate grill, watching carefully and turning often so they do not brown unevenly.

Use immediately or, as long as they are quite dry, store in an airtight jar.

CROSTINI

Cut diagonal 1cm-thick slices of french bread or bread rolls. Brush lightly on both sides with olive oil or a mixture of olive oil and pesto. Sprinkle with a little parmesan if you like. Grill or bake in one layer until lightly browned, as for croutons, but probably for a little longer. Times depend on the moistness of the bread – watch carefully to prevent burning.

TOASTED SPLIT ROLLS

Split rolls and brush cut surface with same mixture as used for crostini. Grill until cut surface is golden brown, turn and grill bases slightly. Serve immediately.

MOUSETRAPS

Very thinly butter thick or thinly sliced fresh or stale bread. Cut in strips, place close together, buttered side down, then sprinkle with grated tasty cheddar and bake at 150°C for about 30 minutes or until lightly browned. Separate strips if necessary, cool on racks, and eat straight away, or hide in airtight jars for up to 2 weeks!

Creamy Green Pea Soup

VERY EASY VEGETARIAN

FINGER FOODS AND SNACKS

If you are looking at the name of this section and asking 'What do you mean by finger food?', let us explain.

There are often times when you want a snack – something light to eat. This could be mid-morning in the weekend, around lunch time (on any day when you are at home), straight after work, before going out to eat, before you serve dinner to friends, or it could be late at night when hunger pangs strike!

Our finger food is casual and pretty quickly made, usually from food which happens to be in the store cupboard, refrigerator or freezer.

It can often be made ahead – or made so that you can eat some of it now, and put the rest in the refrigerator for later.

It tastes good, is reasonably priced, and is made from ingredients which should be part of a good eating pattern. Try to get into the habit of eating snacks which have nutritional advantages, instead of grabbing a chocolate bar, or fat-laden takeways.

Of course, there are some high quality, nutritious 'instant snacks' on sale in your supermarket. The first that come to mind are dried fruit, nuts and seeds, alone or in interesting mixtures in 'Bulk Foods' departments. These are so good that we have not included recipes for making your own!

Some of our other favourite finger foods can be found in our earlier books, *Meals Without Meat* and *Meals Without Red Meat*.

Enjoy our finger foods, from toast toppings for mid-morning sustenance to savoury muffins for lunch, and wedges, dips and Dukkah later in the day!

Marinated Mushrooms (see page 35)
and Crostini with assorted toppings (see page 49)

TWICE-BAKED POTATO SKINS

Loved for their crispness, twice-baked potato skins are made from potatoes which have been previously baked whole.

If baking only a few potatoes, microwave them on full power, allowing about 10 minutes for 400g, or 18–20 minutes for 800g. Bake larger numbers of potatoes on an oven rack at 200°C for 45–60 minutes.

In either case, potatoes are cooked when they 'give' slightly when squeezed (use a cloth to prevent burns).

Quarter medium-sized baked potatoes lengthways. Cut bigger potatoes lengthways into sixths. Scoop or cut out flesh, leaving 5–8mm of potato on skins. (Use flesh for other recipes.)

Brush with olive or other oil, then season with salt and pepper or your favourite seasoning mix. (Prepare ahead to this stage if you like.)

Bake in one layer in a shallow roasting pan or metal baking pan, at 230°C for 15–20 minutes, or until crisp with golden-brown edges. Sprinkle with a little grated cheese, or chopped olives etc., if desired before lifting off the baking pan.

Serve hot, with your favourite dip, sweet chilli sauce, sour cream (plain or flavoured with chopped herbs or pesto), etc.

JACKET WEDGES

These easy-to-cook, tasty and filling snacks seem to be popular with all age groups. Ring the changes by adding different spices to flavour them, then serve them with bought or homemade dips – the sky's the limit!

FOR 3–4 SERVINGS:

4 large potatoes (about 1kg)
3 tablespoons olive oil
1 tablespoon Kikkoman soy sauce
1 teaspoon (1–2 cloves) minced garlic
1 teaspoon ground cumin
1 tablespoon grated parmesan cheese
1 tablespoon flour

Scrub but do not peel the potatoes. Cut each into halves, quarters, then eighths lengthways. Put the prepared wedges into a bowl of cold water and leave to stand while you mix together the olive oil, soy sauce, garlic, cumin, parmesan cheese and flour in another bowl.

Drain potatoes and pat completely dry between several layers of paper towels. Drop the dried potatoes into the seasoning mixture, then, using your fingers, gently turn them in it to coat them thoroughly.

Twice-Baked Potato Skins

Lie wedges in one layer on baking paper in a large shallow roasting dish or other baking pan, or in a baking pan with a good non-stick finish, drizzled with a little oil.

Bake at 200–220°C for 35–40 minutes, or until tender and golden brown, turning after 20 minutes.

If you like, sprinkle with a little salt, seasoned salt, and/or grated cheddar cheese before lifting off the baking pan. (We have found that wedges salted before cooking are not as crisp.)

Serve straight away, with dips such as guacamole, salsa, satay sauce, or sour cream, as snacks or appetisers.

VARIATIONS: Use different herbs and spices.

SAVOURY EGG TOPPING

This is one of Alison's favourite 'comfort foods'. On crackers or crostini, in sandwiches, filled rolls or rollups, it tastes just the way really good egg filling should! What a treat!

4 hard-boiled eggs, still warm
2 tablespoons milk
1 tablespoon butter, at room temperature
1/4 cup finely chopped chives, spring onions or parsley
1/4–1/2 teaspoon salt
pepper to taste

Shell the eggs and put with the other ingredients into a food processor and process until smooth, adding salt and pepper to taste. Or mash the eggs with a fork then mix well with the remaining ingredients, adding salt and pepper to taste. Cover and refrigerate until you want it, for up to 3–4 days. The mixture may seem firm when taken straight from the refrigerator, but will soften as it warms.

Spread on crackers or crostini, then top savouries with a fresh herb sprig, a slice of olive, gherkin, or tomato wedge if you like.

NOTE: You don't need to butter the bread when using this for sandwiches. Mayonnaise or sour cream in the filling will spoil its flavour.

BOILING EGGS:
To boil eggs, bring to the boil enough water to cover eggs. Pierce the blunt end with a needle or pointed knife to stop the egg cracking during cooking. Gently lower the eggs into the boiling water. For soft-boiled eggs allow 5–6 minutes, or for hard-boiled eggs 8–12 minutes. Eight-minute eggs have a firm but brighter and moister yolk (see page 62), 10–12 minute hard-boiled eggs are better for mashing or stuffing. Cool hard-boiled eggs in cold water straight after cooking to stop a dark ring forming between yolk and white.

STUFFED EGGS

These disappear fast whenever we make them. We serve them for lunch with salady things, or with other snacks before a vegetable main course for evening entertaining.

To stop egg shells splitting as you boil them, tap a tiny hole in the rounded end with a metal skewer or any sharp, metal tool. Simmer eggs (covered in water) for about 12 minutes, then stand them in cold water until cool enough to handle, tap gently all over to crack the shells evenly, then peel off shells. Halve lengthways and gently lift out the yolks. Mash these with a fork, adding ½ teaspoon butter per egg, and enough milk to soften them to smooth, spoonable consistency. Add a few capers, chopped herbs or olives if you like, season carefully, then spoon the filling back into the whites.

GOOD OLD ONION DIP

Dips like this have been around for a long time, but are still quick, easy, and very popular. They are suitable for vegetarians as long as you read the soup packet carefully, and choose a brand which does not contain animal products.

FOR ABOUT A CUP:

1 packet (about 55g) onion soup
250g carton low-fat or regular sour cream

Stir the soup mix and sour cream together with a fork until no lumps of powder remain. Leave to stand for at least half an hour, until the pieces of onion soften.

Use straight away or cover and refrigerate for up to 2 days, thinning with milk or yoghurt if it thickens too much.

Serve with a colourful selection of crisp, cold vegetable pieces, slices or sticks. Suitable vegetables include carrots, celery, red and green peppers, cauliflower, young green beans, button mushrooms, radishes, daikon, young turnips, tender asparagus heads and snow peas.

To crisp vegetables, wash, cut up as desired, rinse with cold water leaving a little remaining, then refrigerate in sealed plastic bags until required.

VARIATIONS: Replace half or more of the sour cream with plain, unsweetened yoghurt. Stir one or more of the following into the dip: chopped chives, spring onions, parsley or other fresh herbs, curry powder or paste, pesto, finely chopped walnuts, chopped roasted peanuts, chutney or Tabasco sauce.

ZESTY RED BEAN DIP

I like to take a can of red beans from my store cupboard and make this lively dip with it in just a few minutes. Its flavour depends on the seasonings added, so use more or less, to suit your own taste.

FOR 1¾ CUPS:

1 large clove garlic
¼ red onion or 2 spring onions
¼ cup roughly chopped parsley
2 tablespoons roughly chopped coriander leaves
1 teaspoon ground cumin
2 teaspoons pickled Jalapeno peppers
2 teaspoons lime (or lemon) juice
1 tablespoon tomato paste
2 tablespoons olive oil, optional
400g can kidney beans, drained
bean liquid, to thin mixture

Put the peeled, roughly chopped garlic and onion, or the spring onion stems and leaves cut in 2 cm lengths, into a food processor with the parsley, coriander leaves, cumin, Jalapeno pepper slices (from a jar) and lime or lemon juice. Chop finely, then clean the sides of the processor and add the tomato paste and olive oil and process again, briefly.

Drain the bean liquid into a suitable container, then add the drained beans and process until mixed but not completely smooth. Add enough bean liquid to thin the dip to the consistency you like, then taste to see if it needs more seasoning. You may need none – it depends on the seasoning of the beans and the peppers. If bland, add a little salt and more lime or lemon juice, or more tomato paste. If it is too zesty, add enough sour cream to 'soften' the flavours.

Serve with corn chips, crisp vegetable strips or toasted wedges of flour tortillas. Refrigerate, using within 3 days.

For extra-easy pesto dips, simply stir 2–3 tablespoons of your favourite pesto through 1 cup of sour cream, cream cheese or plain unsweetened yoghurt. Thin with milk if required and adjust seasoning if necessary.

Serve these dips with raw vegetables, potato wedges (see page 27), corn chips, crostini or bruschetta (see page 49), melba toast, crisp-baked pita bread wedges (see page 32) or baked, grilled or fried tortilla wedges.

Stuffed Eggs, and Good Old Onion Dip

EASY SALSA FRESCA

You can make this fresh-tasting salsa all year round. It's best the day it's made, but can be refrigerated for up to 3 days.

¼ red onion or 2 spring onions
1 large clove garlic
1–2 tablespoons pickled Jalapeno peppers
1 tablespoon liquid from jar of Jalapeno peppers
½ teaspoon ground cumin
½ teaspoon oreganum
400g can whole tomatoes in juice or 4 large fresh red
   tomatoes, roughly chopped
½–1 teaspoon salt
½–1 teaspoon sugar
2–3 tablespoons chopped coriander leaves, optional

Chop the first six ingredients together in a food processor. (Use more peppers for extra hotness.) Add tomatoes and process until mixed but chunky. Add salt and sugar to taste (fresh tomatoes need more than canned tomatoes) and add coriander leaves if you have them. Leave for about half an hour before using.

Use as a dip with corn chips, mix with mashed avocado to make an easy Guacamole, or spoon over poached eggs (Alison's favourite!) and Mexican mixtures.

NOTE: Chop vegetables by hand if you don't have a food processor.

GREEN PEA GUACAMOLE

If you keep an 'emergency' packet of frozen peas in the freezer, you can use it to make this surprisingly good, brilliant green, nearly instant dip if the need arises.

MAKES ABOUT 2 CUPS:

¼ cup roughly chopped coriander leaves
1 tablespoon chopped pickled Jalapeno peppers (from a jar)
1 tablespoon liquid from jar of Jalapeno peppers
½ teaspoon ground cumin
1 teaspoon herb, onion or garlic salt
2 spring onions, roughly chopped
1 tablespoon lime or lemon juice
400–500g frozen peas (baby peas if possible)
about 3 tablespoons olive oil

Put the first seven ingredients in a food processor, Use fresh lime juice, the (unsweetened) lime juice in plastic bottles, or fresh lemon juice.

Partly thaw the peas and get rid of any ice by putting them in a sieve (in several batches) and running hot water over them.

Process the nearly thawed (uncooked) peas with the other ingredients until evenly chopped and fairly smooth, adding the oil while processing. Taste and add more flavourings if you want a more highly seasoned dip.

Use immediately as a dip for corn chips, potato chips, wedges or toasted pita bread, or spread on crostini, crisp crackers, etc., and eat straight away. Refrigerate leftovers in a covered container, for up to 24 hours.

EASY GUACAMOLE

A dollop of this guacamole will improve almost any snack – so grab a ready-to-use avocado (its flesh will 'give' slightly at this stage) whenever you see a nice one in the supermarket!

1 ripe avocado
2–3 tablespoons Easy Salsa Fresca (opposite)
   or 2 tablespoons lemon juice
1 finely chopped spring onion
¼ teaspoon salt
Tabasco sauce
chopped coriander leaves, optional

Cut around the centre of the avocado lengthways, then gently twist the two halves apart. Chop a sharp knife into the stone and twist it to remove the stone.

Spoon the flesh into a bowl, scraping out the greenest flesh close to the shell. Mash with a fork, and add the salsa or the remaining ingredients, using quantities to suit your taste. Use immediately or cover with cling film touching the surface and leave for no longer than an hour before using.

Use as a dip for corn chips, as a topping for Mexican foods, crackers, crostini, and in other ways you like.

AVOCADO TIPS:
To halve an avocado cut lengthways around the centre into the stone, gently twist the halves in opposite directions and lift apart. To remove the stone, chop a knife into it, then twist the knife and lift out the stone. For quick chunks, simply scoop out pieces of flesh with a spoon. Remember the dark green layer just inside the skin gives mashed mixtures good colour. Scraped or roughly mashed avocado is an ideal first food for babies.

Easy Salsa Fresca, and Easy Guacamole

CRISPED FLAT BREADS

The growing number of flat breads on the market, including pita bread, various tortillas, Middle Eastern flat breads, Indian naan, and mountain bread, make interesting and varied snacks.

When fresh and soft, these flat breads may be easily rolled up or folded around various fillings but, if they stand around too long, they tend to crack when folded or rolled, especially when cold.

Fresh or not quite so fresh, they may be left flat, cut into smaller pieces and baked, grilled or heated in a pan until crisp. They then make great dippers, or crisp edible small 'plates' on which other foods may be piled.

Thin flour tortillas make excellent crisps, cut into squares, rectangles or wedge shapes, or sometimes heated in large rounds, then broken into small pieces for dipping.

Brush both surfaces lightly but evenly with a little (olive) oil.

Heat in a heavy, dry, preheated pan, about 3–4 minutes per side, until there are darker flecks on each side (the tortilla will become crisper as it cools on a rack) OR

Heat for about the same time under a grill until golden brown, turning after 2 minutes OR

Heat on an oven tray at 180°C for about the same time, until evenly golden brown, without turning.

Cool on a rack.

QUESADILLAS

We keep flour tortillas in the freezer so we can make these crisp savouries at short notice. With crusted brown cheesy toppings flecked with colourful tomato and avocado they are irresistible.

Lie flour tortillas on a grill pan or oven tray. Brush edges lightly with olive oil. Cover with grated cheese then chop several of the following into pea-sized pieces: red onions, olives, tomatoes, red or green peppers, brown flat mushrooms, avocado. Sprinkle these on evenly, add some canned Mexican bean mixtures if you like, then put some more cheese on top.

Grill 5–8 cm from the heat or bake at 180°C for 5–8 minutes, until the cheese melts and browns slightly and the edges are brown and crisp.

QUESADILLA 'SANDWICHES'

To make these thin, cheese-filled crisp tortilla sandwiches, lightly oil two flour tortillas. With the oiled side out, put grated cheese (and extra flavourings as used in quesadillas if you like) between them. Cut into quarters before cooking, for easier turning and handling, and pan-cook, or grill (turning once) or bake at 180°C for 5–8 minutes or until lightly browned and crisp.

Cut into smaller wedges soon after cooking, and eat while still fairly crisp. (We think they are just right, not too crisp and not too soft, after 5–10 minutes.)

Eat just as they are, serve with soup, or use as dippers, especially for guacamole and salsa.

MEXICAN PIZZAS

For a quick and easy snack, spread canned Taco Beans, Chilli Beans or other bean and tomato mixtures on oiled or plain pita breads or flour tortillas, add sliced brown mushrooms, avocados, etc., if you have them, top the lot with your favourite cheese and grill or bake at 180°C until the toppings have heated through and the cheese has melted.

TOSTADAS

These are fun to eat, even if a bit messy! Fry flour or corn tortillas in about 5mm of oil for 1–2 minutes per side, until lightly browned and quite crisp, but not so crisp that they fragment at the first bite! Pile in a cloth-lined basket and let your friends put one on a plate and pile various toppings on it. Provide warmed (canned) Taco Beans or other Mexican style beans, shredded lettuce, and several of the following: chopped tomatoes, chopped spring onion, grated cheese, salsa, guacamole or sliced avocado, sour cream , chopped coriander leaves. Make sure you provide paper napkins, since these require some skill to eat with the fingers, and provide forks, in case they are needed!

Wraps are fashionable finger food. To make them, simply wrap or fold any of your favourite fillings in a warmed flour tortilla or other very thin flat bread. Unlike burritos, which contain Mexican-style fillings, wrap fillings can come from anywhere! Suitable fillings include: leftovers, shredded or grated salad vegetables and cheese, cooked asparagus or other ideas from this page. For easy eating, enclose wraps securely in paper or foil to prevent drips.

Quesadillas

ALISON'S DUKKAH

Dukkah is a highly flavoured mixture of nuts and spices which originated in ancient Egypt. The crushed (but not powdered) mixtures were traditionally made to suit the tastes of its makers, and were served in shallow bowls. Pieces of good, firm, crusty bread were dipped in olive oil, then Dukkah, and eaten as a snack or meal.

Alison's Dukkah mixture is delicious used in this way and also makes a 'Very Easy' last minute flavouring for salads, soups, and plainly cooked vegetables, for a couple of months after it is initially made. For this reason, we have included it here.

FOR 2 CUPS OF DUKKAH:

1/2 **cup sesame seeds**
1/2 **cup sunflower seeds**
1/2 **cup pumpkin seeds**
1 **cup blanched almonds**
1/4 **cup cumin seeds**
1/4 **cup coriander seeds**
1 1/2 **teaspoons rock salt**
1 **tablespoon (ground) paprika**
1 1/2 **teaspoons (ground) turmeric**

Heat the oven to 180°C. Put the seeds and almonds in to roast, in separate foil dishes and/or pie plates etc., in the order given. We find that the first few take longer than those listed last. Watch carefully, checking them at least every 5 minutes, and take out each container when the seeds have darkened a little (but not a lot) and have an appetising aroma. (As a guide, most will take about 10 minutes, but sesame and sunflower seeds usually take longer.)

Leave to cool, then grind with the salt, paprika and turmeric, in one or two batches in a food processor, using the pulse button. The final mixture should have a grainy texture – it should not be an oily powder.

Store in airtight jars in a cool cupboard. Although it will gradually lose some flavour on long storage, it will taste very good for up to 3 months.

NOTE: Sprinkle Dukkah over potatoes, green beans, or other cooked vegetables which would be improved by its added colour, flavour and texture. Sprinkle on cubed or sliced raw tomato or cucumber for an easy salad.

MARINATED MUSHROOMS

If you plan to have a few friends around, and are serving drinks before a meal, include a bowl of marinated mushrooms (or a flat plate containing drained marinated mushrooms, already speared with cocktail sticks) with other finger food. They are sure to prove quite irresistible to many people.

about 300g small, tightly closed button mushrooms
1/4 **cup wine vinegar**
1 **teaspoon balsamic vinegar, optional**
1 **teaspoon (1–2 cloves) minced garlic**
1 **teaspoon oreganum**
1/2 **teaspoon salt**
1 **teaspoon sugar**
1 **tablespoon tomato paste**
1/2 **cup olive oil**

Brush the mushrooms clean if necessary. Trim the stem level with the cap of the mushrooms if you like, then put them aside. Halve large button mushrooms if desired.

Measure the remaining ingredients into a small pot, bring them to the boil, stirring to mix everything, then add the mushrooms, stirring until they soften and are covered with the hot liquid. Simmer for about 3 minutes, then transfer to a jar, making sure that the liquid covers them. Cover and leave to cool.

Serve hot, warm or at room temperature within 3 days, refrigerating meantime.

NOTES: Olive oil turns cloudy when refrigerated. It will clear again when warmed a little.

Toss remaining liquid through pasta or whisk a little mustard into it and use as a salad dressing, if desired.

Sliced marinated mushrooms make great toppings for pizzas. **For very easy individual pizzas,** halve hamburger buns or use small round pita breads. Spread with sun-dried tomato pesto or tomato paste, then add a selection (two or three is usually enough!) of your favourite toppings and sprinkle generously with grated cheese. Bake at 200°C or grill until the cheese bubbles and browns, then serve immediately.

Alison's Dukkah

EASY CHEESY MUFFINS

These are the easiest muffins we make, and also one of our most popular varieties. Make the basic formula and sit back and wait for the compliments, or add extra flavourings to create your own personal speciality! For example, stir in some pizza garnishes and present your friends with Cheesy Pizza Muffins for lunch!

FOR 12 MEDIUM-SIZED MUFFINS:

2 cups self-raising flour
2 cups (200g) grated tasty cheese
1 large egg
1 cup lager or beer

Toss the flour and grated cheese together in a large bowl, using a fork.

In another bowl, again using the fork, beat the egg enough to thoroughly mix the white and yolk. Add the lager or beer (which can be flat or bubbly), stir to mix briefly, then pour the mixture onto the flour and cheese. Fold together until most of the flour is dampened, but do not keep mixing until the mixture is smooth.

Spoon the mixture into 12 buttered or sprayed medium-sized muffin pans. Bake at 220°C for 10–15 minutes, until nicely browned, and until the centres spring back when pressed. Leave to stand in the tins for 3–4 minutes, until they will lift out easily.

Serve warm or cold the day they are made, or reheat the next day.

VARIATIONS: Add one or several of the following to the beaten egg: $\frac{1}{2}$ cup chopped fresh tomatoes or $\frac{1}{4}$ cup sun-dried tomatoes, half an avocado cut in small cubes, $\frac{1}{4}$ cup sautéed chopped mushrooms, 2 tablespoons chopped fresh herbs or 2 tablespoons of your favourite pesto.

ZUCCHINI AND PARMESAN MUFFINS

When Simon invented these muffins, we couldn't believe how good they were! They are light textured and pretty, flecked with pale green, and perfect for summer lunches and for picnics. They are also a boon for the families of zucchini growers!

FOR 12 MEDIUM-SIZED MUFFINS:

2 cups flour
4 teaspoons baking powder
$\frac{1}{2}$ teaspoon salt
black pepper to taste
1 cup grated tasty cheese
$\frac{1}{4}$ cup grated parmesan cheese
$\frac{3}{4}$ cup milk
2 eggs
3 zucchini (250g altogether)

Sift or fork together the flour, baking powder and salt in a large bowl. Grind in black pepper to taste (using plenty if you like its flavour) then add the grated cheeses and stir to combine.

In another bowl whisk together the milk and eggs with a fork, then add the unpeeled, grated zucchini. Tip this mixture into the bowl of dry ingredients.

Fold together, taking care not to overmix. As soon as all the flour is moistened (but before the mixture is smooth), spoon the mixture into 12 lightly buttered or sprayed medium-sized muffin pans or 24 mini-muffin pans.

Bake at 210°C for 12–5 minutes, or until the tops are golden and the muffins spring back when pressed in the centre. Leave to stand for 2–3 minutes, then remove from their tins and cool on a rack. Serve cold or warm without buttering, topped with cottage cheese and/or sliced tomatoes if you like.

MUFFIN TIPS:

Muffins, savoury or sweet (see pages 108–111), are great! They are quick to cook and incredibly versatile – if you want to learn how to bake one thing, make it muffins. By following a few simple pointers it is easy to become a muffin 'expert'.

● Once you have combined wet and dry ingredients, never overmix. Always stop mixing while the mixture looks rough and lumpy – it doesn't matter if a little flour is still visible. Overmixing toughens muffins and makes them rise in peaks instead of being gently rounded.

● Muffins often stick to baking pans, so it's best to use pans with a non-stick finish. Clean pans without scratching them and coat with non-stick spray (unless the instructions tell you not to).

● After cooking, let muffins stand in their pans for 3–4 minutes – they will loosen themselves in this time. To remove from the pan, press gently at the edges with your fingers and turn slightly, as soon as the muffin turns freely it can be lifted out.

Easy Cheesy Muffins and Zucchini and Parmesan Muffins

TOPPINGS FOR TOAST

A piece of toast spread with something tasty is a very useful snack at any time of the day or night.

Some of these toppings are quick enough to make on the spot – others may be prepared in the weekend and kept until you want a 'Very Easy' snack. For variety, keep a selection of different types of sliced breads and split rolls in your freezer, toasting them from frozen if necessary.

(Toast rolls or unevenly thick breads under the grill or in a double sided grill [see page 8], instead of in a toaster.)

PEANUT HONEY

Make crunchy peanut butter, replacing the cashew nuts in Crunchy Cashew Butter (see opposite page) with peanuts. Add to the warm nut mixture about 2 tablespoons of honey. Process until blended. Keep in a jar at room temperature for several weeks. Spread lavishly on warm, unbuttered toast and top with crisp slices of apple, with sliced pear or banana.

AVOCADO TOPPING

Make this just before you want to eat it, since it browns if left standing for long. Roughly mash with a fork 1 medium-sized avocado with 2 teaspoon of lemon juice. Serve on freshly toasted bread without butter. Top with chopped spring onions, chives, basil or coriander leaves, with tomato salsa, or with thick slices of tomato. Grind black pepper over the lot.

CHOCOLATE HAZELNUT SPREAD

Bake 1 cup of hazelnuts at 180°C for about 10 minutes, or until the nut flesh is very lightly browned, then rub in a teatowel to remove their skins. While still hot, place nuts in a food processor with 2 tablespoons castor sugar and mix until finely chopped.

Melt 100g cooking chocolate with 2 tablespoons oil in a pot taking care not to overheat, then add to the nuts and process until fairly smooth.

This will keep for several weeks at room temperature. Spread thickly on unbuttered toast and top with slices of banana.

COTTAGE CHEESE AND TOMATOES

Toast a bagel, English muffin, halved roll, or thick slice of wholemeal bread. Spread generously with your favourite cottage cheese and top with slices of tomato. This is one of the nicest ways to serve garden-fresh tomatoes. Garnish with basil, snowpea shoots, alfalfa sprouts, etc. if you like.

BASIL BUTTER

Cut 100g butter into cubes and soften in the microwave for 20 seconds. Add 2 tablespoons of basil pesto and mix together. Refrigerate for up to 1 week.

Serve at room temperature. Spread thinly on hot toast and serve as is or with sliced tomatoes or avocados.

TUTTI-FRUTTI SPREAD

Heat $1/2$ cup Fruit Medley (mixed dried fruit) in $1/4$ cup orange juice in the microwave for 2 minutes on full power. Stir in 2 teaspoons sugar and cook for 1 minute longer.

Stir in $1/2$ cup of cream cheese, and $1/4$ cup chopped, roasted cashew nuts or almonds if you like. Serve on toasted bagels or bread. Refrigerate for up to 1 week.

NOTE: You can buy Fruit Medley from the bulk foods department of some supermarkets. It contains chopped dried apples, pears, peaches, raisins, and sultanas.

CRUNCHY CASHEW BUTTER

Warm 1 cup of roasted cashew nuts in a microwave or regular oven, then process in a food processor or blender with 2 tablespoons of olive, canola, or other oil. Spread generously on unbuttered toast. Eat like this or top with fresh pear slices.

VARIATION: Use roasted (but never raw) peanuts or other nuts to make other flavourful nut butters.

ALL-IN-ONE CHEESE SPREAD

Melt 100g butter in a pot, then stir in 2 teaspoons flour and 1 teaspoon prepared mustard. Add $1/2$ cup milk and bring to the boil, stirring constantly. Stir in 2 cups grated cheese and 2 teaspoons wine vinegar and heat only until cheese melts.

Remove from heat and stir in 1 large egg. Heat briefly until mixture thickens, then stand the pot in cold water, stirring frequently until mixture is cool.

Refrigerate for up to 2 weeks. Spread on hot, unbuttered toast. Nice topped with sliced tomato.

CINNAMON SUGAR

Shake together in a screw-topped jar $1/4$ cup brown sugar, $1/4$ cup white sugar, and 1 tablespoon cinnamon. Sprinkle on hot buttered toast, plain, or spread with sliced bananas. Eat as is, or heat under grill until bubbly.

This keeps for a couple of months in an airtight jar.

VERY EASY VEGETARIAN
SALADS AND SIDES

We think that many people now often plan meals in terms of one main cooked dish per meal, with perhaps one cooked accompaniment. In this situation, a salad and some bread will make your meal much more interesting and appealing, as well as adding contrasting texture, extra colour, and important nutrients.

This section offers a variety of suggestions. When time is very short and your energy levels particularly low, your easiest option is one of our suggested salad vegetables or fruit, with one of our make-ahead dressings from the refrigerator.

When you want a salad which is economical, using vegetables which you can buy once a week, make once and eat twice, we suggest our interesting coleslaw or unusual Oriental pickled vegetables.

Some of our salads are perfect for packed, take-to-work lunches or lazy weekend midday snacks, while others will suit you when you ask friends for a meal.

Because salads won't always solve your 'serve with' problems, you'll find some suggestions on ways to cook and/or serve other useful accompaniments including rice (white and brown), other grains, pasta mixtures, potatoes, and couscous.

We hope that you will make yourself familiar with a number of the recipes here, and enjoy eating the results. In doing so you will be adding more fruit, vegetables and grain-based foods to your daily meals, and following important dietary guidelines as well.

Birds Nest Salad (see page 44)

SALADS AND DRESSINGS

An interesting salad is often needed to add colour, crunch, and a dash of flavour to a main course. Salads don't have to be complicated – in fact, simple salads are sometimes better than those which contain many ingredients.

Fruits and vegetables have many very important health protecting qualities. Many of us do not eat the minimum of five servings, daily. If you feel that you should increase your fruit and vegetable intake, make a point of eating more salads.

Our fastest salads are made of one vegetable, a tub of mesclun (mixed baby salad vegetables) or a bag of sprouts or undressed coleslaw from the supermarket, tossed in a made-ahead dressing from the refrigerator.

Try several of our easy dressings, drizzling them over single vegetables, then try mixtures of two, three or even more of the vegetables listed below.

Don't limit yourself to raw vegetables, but use warm or cold cooked vegetables and raw fruit on occasion. Here are some suggestions of suitable salad 'base' ingredients, but we are sure you can think of more.

raw apple cubes (toss in dressing before they brown)
avocado halves, slices or cubes
lightly cooked asparagus spears
lightly cooked green beans, chopped
beansprouts, pea sprouts, sunflower sprouts, etc.
beetroot, especially baby, canned
shredded cabbage
cauliflower florets
thinly sliced or lightly cooked sliced celery
shredded raw carrots or sliced cooked carrots
coleslaw mixes (undressed)
corn kernels, roasted, boiled, canned or frozen
kiwifruit slices or cubes
cooked sliced kumara
lettuce, in chunky pieces, torn or sliced
mesclun (baby salad leaves)
raw button mushrooms, sliced or marinated (see page 35)
raw pears, sliced (toss in dressing to stop browning)
peas, cooked
raw sugarpeas in their pods, or snowpeas
peppers, raw or roasted, all colours
waxy cooked potatoes
radishes
sliced spinach leaves
swede, shredded
raw small or large tomatoes
watercress sprigs or leaves
zucchini, lightly cooked or raw

FRENCH DRESSING

This is a good, basic all-purpose dressing which you can put together in a few minutes and keep in your refrigerator. The mustard in it is important, since it stops the dressing separating.

Use it just as it is, or add other flavourings to part of it, reading the recipes below for suggestions. We use it on leafy salads and warm or cold cooked vegetable salads.

¼ cup olive (or other) oil
2 teaspoons wine vinegar
½ teaspoon balsamic vinegar or extra wine vinegar
1 teaspoon prepared mustard
¼ teaspoon salt
1 teaspoon sugar
1 tablespoon water

Refrigerate for up to a week.

ITALIAN DRESSING

Shake the ingredients for French Dressing and 1 teaspoon tomato paste together in a screw-topped jar. Taste to see whether the dressing has a definite tomato flavour. If not, add another teaspoon of tomato paste and shake again. Add another tablespoon of water if the paste thickens the dressing more than you want it to.

This dressing is particularly good used with cooked vegetables, salads, on avocado halves, cottage cheese, and on pasta salads.

HERBED DRESSING

Shake the ingredients for French Dressing with 1–2 tablespoons very finely chopped fresh herbs. Use one or more herbs, depending on your taste and what is available. Replace the salt with ½ teaspoon of herb salt or garlic, onion or celery salt if you like.

Suitable herbs include parsley, chives, dill, tarragon, thyme, and rosemary.

PESTO DRESSING

Add 1–2 tablespoons basil pesto or any other pesto to the French Dressing above, then shake well. Use within 24 hours.

OR Shake or stir together ¼ cup of olive oil with 1–2 tablespoons pesto, 1 teaspoon wine vinegar or lemon juice and add salt to taste. Use immediately.

Stir these dressings into cooked vegetable salads, rice or pasta salads and leafy salads. Alter proportions to suit your taste, taking into consideration the different flavour strengths of different kinds of pesto.

TEX-MEX DRESSING

We use this assertive dressing to liven up many gently flavoured foods. We spoon it into avocado halves, use it to top baked potatoes, drop spoonfuls onto poached eggs, stir it into canned drained beans to make spicy bean salads, and spread it on bread rolls before we add cheese and salad vegetables.

FOR ¾ CUP DRESSING:

½ cup olive oil
1 teaspoon ground cumin
1 teaspoon salt
1 teaspoon sugar
½ teaspoon dried oreganum
½ teaspoon paprika
¼–½ teaspoon chilli paste
1–2 cloves garlic, very finely chopped
2 teaspoons prepared smooth mustard
1 tablespoon tomato paste
1 tablespoon wine vinegar
2 tablespoons boiling water

Measure the first seven ingredients into a jar with a screw-topped lid and shake well to mix.

Mix the garlic, mustard, tomato paste and wine vinegar in a cup or small bowl. Stir in the boiling water to make a smooth paste, then transfer to the jar holding the other ingredients and stir well, then shake thoroughly until smooth and thick.

Leave to stand for at least 30 minutes before using. Refrigerate for up to a week.

SESAME DRESSING

This strongly flavoured dressing is addictive! It turns bought packages of cole slaw or the simplest coleslaw vegetables into something exciting, but also dresses tomato, sprout, mesclun, cooked vegetable and pasta salads well, too. It keeps well and may be refrigerated for weeks. For a milder dressing use only 1 tablespoon sesame oil.

FOR ¾ CUP DRESSING:

¼ cup canola oil
2 tablespoons sesame oil
2 tablespoons wine vinegar
1 tablespoon lemon or lime juice
2 tablespoons sugar
1 tablespoon Thai sweet chilli sauce
1 tablespoon prepared mustard
1 teaspoon salt
1 teaspoon balsamic vinegar, if available

Measure all ingredients into a screw-topped jar and shake together. Use about 2 teaspoons dressing to 1 cup of compact salad, or 1 teaspoon per cup of salad leaves.

SPICY YOGHURT DRESSING

Stir this versatile dressing through chopped celery, chopped or sliced cucumber, sliced firm bananas or cold, cooked new potatoes. With any of these it makes a good curry accompaniment. As well, spoon it over bean and lentil mixtures, and use it as a dip.

FOR 1 CUP DRESSING:

1 clove fresh garlic, finely chopped
1–2 teaspoons chopped pickled Jalapeno peppers
¼ cup chopped fresh coriander leaves
2 spring onions, finely chopped
1 teaspoon ground cumin
½ teaspoon sugar
½ teaspoon salt
1 cup plain, unsweetened yoghurt

Stir all ingredients together in a bowl, or combine in a blender or food processor. Stand for 30 minutes before use if possible. Refrigerate for up to 24 hours.

TOMATO AND BREAD SALAD

Made with firm, red, flavourful tomatoes, this is an outstanding salad, served alone for lunch or with a light main course which needs livening up! Firm-textured french bread works best but you can use whatever you have.

FOR 4 LARGE SERVINGS:

20cm length french bread
about ¼ cup olive oil
2 teaspoons basil or other pesto, optional
4 ripe red tomatoes
¼ red onion or 2 spring onions
about 20 basil leaves, if available
sprinkling of salt, sugar and black pepper

Cut the french bread in quarters lengthways. Mix the olive oil with the pesto if using it, then brush the surfaces of the bread lightly with some of the oil.

Ten minutes before serving, toast bread under a moderate grill, turning so that all the edges are golden but no surfaces burn.

Chop the tomatoes into 1cm cubes and put in a large salad bowl with the finely chopped onion and the basil leaves, whole or broken up by hand.

Just before serving, cut the warm, browned bread into 15mm lengths. Sprinkle the tomatoes with a little salt, sugar and pepper, toss gently, and when the juices start to run, add the bread cubes, toss to mix, drizzle with the unused oil and serve immediately.

NOTE: Alter amounts of tomato and bread if you like.

BIRDS NEST SALAD

This salad is a talking point – different, interesting and very popular.

FOR 4–6 SERVINGS:

DRESSING:

1 clove garlic, very finely chopped
½ teaspoon chilli paste
1 tablespoon each sugar and sesame oil
1 tablespoon rice vinegar or wine vinegar
2 tablespoons each water and Kikkoman soy sauce

about 50g dry rice vermicelli noodles
oil for frying
about 4 cups mesclun, lettuce or other salad greens
beansprouts, chopped spring onions, etc.
¼ cup chopped coriander leaves
½ cup roughly chopped or halved roasted peanuts

Make the dressing by shaking together the first seven ingredients in a screw-topped jar.

Pull the rice noodles away from the block and cut them into shorter lengths. Heat oil about 1cm deep in a wok or medium-sized pot or pan until one or two noodles dropped in it puff up. Keeping oil at this heat, fry the noodles in small handfuls, turning them with tongs when the under side is puffed. They should be very lightly coloured (but not brown) rather than white. Drain and cool on paper towels. (Make ahead and store for up to an hour in an airtight plastic bag if you like.)

Assemble salad 30 seconds before serving. Toss together the noodles, (dry) salad greens, other salad additions, chopped coriander and the peanuts. Add half the dressing, toss, then taste, adding more if desired.

VARIATION: Semi-vegetarians and non-vegetarians might like to replace the soy sauce in the dressing with fish sauce.

FRUIT SALAD

This salad is a cross between a salad and a fruit salsa.

FOR 4 SERVINGS:

2 apples, pears, or an equivalent amount of fresh pineapple
   or kiwi fruit, bananas, etc.
2 tablespoons unsweetened lime juice
¼ cup olive oil
1 clove garlic, finely chopped
¼ teaspoon each minced red chilli and salt
¼ cup chopped fresh coriander
1 cup sunflower, rocket or other crunchy sprouts
about 2 tablespoons chopped walnuts or toasted almonds

A short time before serving prepare the fruit, removing cores, etc. but not the skin of apples or pears. Slice into the salad bowl. Prepare other fruit suitably.

Mix together the lime juice, oil, garlic, minced chilli, and salt. Turn the fruit gently in the dressing, sprinkle the coriander leaves, sprouts and chopped nuts through it or over the top and serve immediately.

'BROCAULI' SALAD

You can eat this as soon as you coat the cooked vegetables with dressing, or leave it to stand for up to 24 hours.

FOR 4 SERVINGS:

200–250g prepared broccoli
250–300g prepared cauliflower
½ cup olive oil
¼ cup white wine vinegar
1 clove garlic, very finely chopped
1 teaspoon dried oreganum
1–2 teaspoons prepared mustard, optional
salt and freshly ground black pepper

Cut the broccoli and cauliflower into bite-sized pieces, peeling off and discarding any tough outer skin, then boil in a little lightly salted water, in a covered pot until tender-crisp. Drain, cool to room temperature in very cold water, then drain again and refrigerate in a plastic bag if not using immediately.

To make the dressing: Combine the oil and vinegar in a screw-topped jar, and add the fresh garlic, crumbled dried oreganum and mustard. Shake well, then add salt and pepper to taste.

To keep the broccoli's green colour, toss the cooled broccoli and cauliflower in the dressing just before serving. For more flavour, but olive-coloured broccoli, add the dressing to the vegetables as soon as both are prepared and leave to stand.

CARROT SALAD

Use this tasty carrot mixture as a salad, relish or sandwich filling.

FOR 4 SERVINGS:

2 large carrots
1 spring onion
2–4 tablespoons finely chopped mint or coriander leaves
1 teaspoon finely grated root ginger
2 tablespoons lemon juice

Shred the carrots coarsely. Toss with the finely chopped spring onion, the chopped mint or coriander leaves, ginger and lemon juice. Use immediately, or refrigerate in a plastic bag, for up to 2 days.

SPICED TOMATO (AND CUCUMBER) SALAD

This salad needs no dressing. With or without the cucumber it is a good salad for many purposes but is especially useful as an accompaniment for curries and Mexican foods which do not contain tomatoes.

FOR 4–6 SERVINGS:

3–4 red, firm, flavourful tomatoes
½ telegraph cucumber, optional
2 spring onions or ¼ red onion
1 tablespoon sugar
1–2 teaspoons ground cumin
½ teaspoon salt
chopped coriander leaves, optional

Cut the tomatoes into neat 1cm cubes. If using, cut the unpeeled cucumber into cubes the same size. Slice the spring onions thinly or finely chop the red onion. Place prepared vegetables in a serving dish, sprinkle with the sugar, cumin and salt and toss gently. (Use the smaller amount of cumin if not using the cucumber.) Sprinkle with coriander leaves if desired and serve chilled or at room temperature.

AVOCADO WITH MEDITERRANEAN DRESSING

Give avocados star status with this dressing!

FOR 4 SERVINGS:

DRESSING:
2 tablespoons olive oil
¼ cup pine nuts
4 sun-dried tomatoes, chopped
2 teaspoons balsamic or wine vinegar
1 clove garlic, very finely chopped
¼ teaspoon salt
freshly ground black pepper to taste

2 ripe avocados

Warm a little of the olive oil in a frying pan, add the pine nuts and heat until golden brown. Add the rest of the oil and the remaining ingredients, then put aside until required.

Just before serving, halve the avocados, cutting around them, and twisting the halves gently. Remove the stones by chopping a sharp knife into the stone and twisting the knife. Spoon dressing into the cavities and serve promptly.

Avocado with Mediterranean Dressing

SWEET AND SOUR VEGETABLE MIXTURES

Try this unusual, strongly flavoured dressing in three different ways, to ring the changes with useful, inexpensive vegetables which will keep for at least a week in your refrigerator, e.g. spring onions, cabbage, carrots and celery.

ALISON'S SWEET AND SOUR SESAME DRESSING

2 tablespoons white wine vinegar
2 tablespoons rice vinegar or more wine vinegar
2 tablespoons lemon juice
2 tablespoons sugar
2 tablespoons sesame oil
2 tablespoons canola oil
1–2 tablespoons Thai Sweet Chilli Sauce
1½ teaspoons salt
about 1 tablespoon grated root ginger
2 large cloves garlic, crushed or grated

Shake everything together in a screw-topped jar and use in the following recipes. Refrigerate for up to 2 weeks, shaking before use.

EASY ORIENTAL COLESLAW

Shred cabbage and celery and grate carrot, by hand or in a food processor. Add a few chopped roasted peanuts, and add just enough dressing to moisten the vegetables.

SWEET AND SOUR VEGETABLE STIR-FRY

For 4 large servings, cut a large carrot and a celery stalk into long strips the thickness of matches, and shred about 500g of cabbage thickly. In a large wok stir-fry the carrot and celery in a tablespoon of oil until just wilted, then add the cabbage and toss it with the other vegetables for about a minute. Add about ½ cup of Sesame Dressing and bring to the boil over a high heat, still stirring constantly. Add enough cornflour and water paste to thicken the liquid so that it coats the vegetables, and serve instantly.

ORIENTAL PICKLED VEGETABLES

Cut up carrot, celery and cabbage as for the previous recipe. Cook in the same way, adding only ¼ cup of the prepared dressing. Instead of thickening the mixture, cool the wok in iced water until the vegetables reach room temperature. At this stage stir in another ¼ cup of dressing, and refrigerate the mixture in a covered container for up to 48 hours.

Serve in sandwiches, filled rolls and warmed flour tortillas (with grated cheese).

MEMORABLE COLESLAWS

It's worth learning how to make a good coleslaw for a number of reasons.

Coleslaw doesn't call for anything exotic or expensive, its ingredients will keep in the refrigerator for days, will be available right through the year, and won't cost very much. You can make coleslaw ahead of time and take it to pot-luck meals or picnics. If these reasons are not enough for you, picky eaters may eat coleslaw because they know what it is, and it need never be boring, because you can make so many variations to it.

For basic coleslaw, simply shred quarter of a drum-head cabbage very finely (with a sharp knife or a food-processor slicing blade), coarsely grate a scrubbed carrot or two (with a hand grater or the shredding blade of a food processor), and toss the two together with any of the dressings on pages 42 and 43. Our favourite coleslaw dressing is Sesame Dressing (see page 43).

Other suitable vegetable additions are thinly sliced celery, peppers, cauliflower and spring onions.

Look for packets of just-starting-to-sprout chickpeas, lentils, adzuki and mung beans, and pea sprouts, since these give coleslaw a lovely, slightly nutty flavour.

For sweetness add cubes of unpeeled apple tossed in lemon juice, sultanas, currants or Californian raisins.

Grated cheese always seems a popular addition to basic cabbage, carrot and celery. This variation makes a good filling for pita bread and split rolls, too.

A sprinkling of toasted seeds and nuts makes a change and Two Minute Noodle Coleslaw is always a good talking point! (See instructions below.)

FOR TOASTED SEEDS AND NUTS

Cook in a heavy frying pan over low heat ½ cup each of sunflower seeds, pumpkin seeds and chopped raw (skin on) almonds. Toss them in ½ teaspoon of sesame oil and cook, shaking the pan at intervals, for 5–10 minutes, until the pumpkin seeds look plump. Cool, then store in a screw-topped jar. Sprinkle a few tablespoons into coleslaw when serving.

FOR TWO MINUTE NOODLE COLESLAW

Partially break up the noodles from a packet of Two Minute Noodles. Place on foil and heat under a moderate grill until noodles turn golden brown (1–2 minutes). Break into smaller pieces, store in an airtight container and toss through coleslaw which has been tossed with Sesame Dressing, just moments before it is to be eaten.

NOTE: Don't do this too often since these noodles are usually fried in palm oil (a saturated plant oil) before you get them.

Elizabeth's Favourite Salad

ELIZABETH'S FAVOURITE SALAD

Alison's granddaughters Elizabeth and Jennifer, given the ingredients and sharp knives, make this ever-popular salad willingly and efficiently, at the drop of a hat!

FOR 4 SERVINGS:

1 tablespoon lemon juice
1 teaspoon sugar
¼ teaspoon salt
1 large avocado
2–3 firm, red tomatoes
10cm length telegraph cucumber
about 2 cups of chopped crisp-leaf lettuce
1 or 2 spring onions
1 tablespoon olive oil
pepper to taste

Mix the lemon juice, sugar and salt in the bottom of a fairly large salad bowl. Remove the skin and stone from the avocado, cut into 1 cm cubes and turn gently in the lemon juice without breaking up.

Cut the tomatoes into slices 1cm thick, then into 1cm cubes. Discard excess juice and place pieces on avocado, without tossing. Cut unpeeled cucumber in 1cm cubes and sprinkle over tomato.

Cut a firm, hearty (iceberg) lettuce into 1–2cm squares, without separating the leaves, or romaine hearts into 1cm slices. Slice stems and some spring onion leaves into thin slices and add to the bowl, without mixing.

Cover with cling film and refrigerate for up an hour if not serving immediately. When serving, sprinkle with the olive oil, freshly ground pepper, add a little extra salt if necessary, and toss gently to coat ingredients without bruising or breaking them.

Good with almost any main course, or for lunch.

47

BEAN SALAD

Alison keeps modifying this useful do-ahead salad which she has made for years! It keeps for 2 or 3 days, is a good companion to plain tomatoes or avocados, and a tasty addition to filled rolls.

FOR 3–4 SERVINGS:

310–400g can mixed beans or kidney beans
1/4 red onion, chopped
3 tablespoons olive or canola oil
2 tablespoons wine vinegar
1 tablespoon sugar
1/2 teaspoon ground cumin
1/2 teaspoon salt
about 1 cup chopped peppers (any colour)
1/4 cup chopped celery, optional

Tip beans into a sieve, saving about 2 tablespoons of liquid from the can if possible. Rinse under a tap.

Tip the drained, washed beans into the container in which you will keep the salad and add the next six ingredients. Add the reserved bean liquid or 1 tablespoon of water and mix gently until sugar dissolves.

Cut the peppers and celery into 5mm cubes, stir into the bean mixture and leave for at least 15 minutes before serving. Serve with a slotted spoon, so remaining salad is covered with dressing. Refrigerate for up to 3 days, adding chopped parsley when serving, if desired.

BEAN SPROUTS AND CARROT SALAD

Very satisfying flavours and textures! Assemble just before eating, preparing components ahead if you like.

FOR ABOUT 6 SERVINGS:

3 slices bread, preferably wholemeal
1 tablespoon olive oil
2 large carrots, coarsely grated
1 cup bean or other sprouts
1/2 cup each salted peanuts and sultanas
1/4 cup finely chopped parsley
2 tablespoons olive or other oil
2 teaspoons sesame oil
2 tablespoons lemon juice
1/2 teaspoon salt
1 teaspoon sugar

Cut the bread into 5mm cubes. Heat the oil in a small frying pan, toss the bread cubes in it, then cook until they are crisp and golden brown croutons. Cool and put aside.

Put grated carrots, sprouts, peanuts, sultanas and parsley in a salad bowl. Cover and refrigerate if not needed immediately. Mix second measure of oil, the sesame oil, lemon juice, salt and sugar and put aside.

Just before serving toss half the croutons through the other ingredients, add the dressing and toss again, then sprinkle with the remaining croutons. Serve as a side dish or pack into a pita pocket.

Bean Salad, Bean Sprouts and Carrot Salad

'ON THE SIDE'

We called this chapter 'Salads and Sides' because we felt that these were very important meal accompaniments. (Cooked vegetables are too, but we have written about these at length in Meals Without Meat.*)*

By 'Sides' we mean the extra foods you might serve 'on the side' with your main meal. We consider bread, rice and other grains, pasta, couscous and potatoes to be 'sides' in this context. They are all rich in complex carbohydrates, low in fat, are usually inexpensive, compared with other foods, and are good, popular fillers – the perfect thing to serve to people who have large appetites because they are growing fast, or are exercising more than many of us!

BREAD

In keeping with our 'Very Easy' theme, we decided (rather reluctantly) that we would not include any homemade bread recipes, but we hope that, if you own a bread machine, you will use it often. Putting half a dozen ingredients into a machine and turning it on must surely be considered a 'very easy' way to get good quality, aromatic, fresh and inexpensive bread to serve with, or as a main part of, your meals.

When it comes to buying bread, there are many different and exciting varieties to choose from. Shop around, seeing what is available locally, in the larger supermarkets in your area, and in speciality bread shops. If you find particularly good breads at speciality shops which are not on your way home, buy extra when you do go, then wrap and seal them carefully, and freeze them so they are on hand for special occasions.

We tend to look for more substantial crusty, chewy breads and rolls which have interesting textures and flavours. These may be farmhouse style loaves, long, sour dough french loaves, ciabatta and focaccia or dark rye breads. Other 'ethnic' breads such as naan and other Indian breads, tortillas, and flat 'mountain' breads make interesting meal additions, especially for meals with an ethnic theme.

All bread is good food, but those made using wholemeal flour and kibbled grains have even greater nutritional advantages, especially for vegetarians.

If you can't get interesting firm-textured bread, try the following recipe to add body to softer bread, to serve with soup, salads and mains, or to use as a base for snacks.

CROSTINI/BRUSCHETTA

Cut fresh or slightly stale rolls in half lengthways, or long, thin loaves in 1–2cm thick, diagonal slices. Add 2–3 tablespoons olive oil to 2–3 tablespoons of basil (or other favourite) pesto, (anchovy-free) tapenade or other seasonings. Brush the flavoured oil over the cut surfaces of the bread, add a sprinkling of parmesan cheese if you like, and grill (both sides if necessary) under moderate heat until the edges of the bread are golden brown and crisp.

Serve warm as a side, or top with simple savoury toppings and add a garnish. (In the photo on page 25 basil pesto and sun-dried tomato pesto were mixed with the olive oil, the toppings used were sliced brie, blue brie, marinated mushrooms, sweet 100 tomatoes, fresh dill and sunflower sprouts.

RICE AND OTHER GRAINS

The number of different kinds of rice available in supermarkets has increased considerably in the past few years. If you are not sure which rice to buy and how to cook it, read the packet information and instructions carefully, and follow them precisely.

Long-grained rices do not stick together as shorter grained rices do. Long-grain rices are usually used for accompaniments for wet curries and other 'saucy' dishes while arborio and calrose rices, which have shorter grains, are better for risotto, sushi and thickened puddings.

Basmati and Jasmine rices are termed 'Aromatic'. They cook in a similar time to other long-grain rices, and have a definite (delicious) flavour of their own.

Some rices are given special treatments during processing to shorten their cooking times, or to stop their grains clumping together.

Brown rice, which has not had its outer layers removed, has a nutty flavour and nutritional advantages, but also requires long cooking, usually 2–3 times as much as white rice. Both short and long-grain brown rice stay in separate grains after cooking.

Rice mixtures contain two or more different types or rice. They should be cooked according to the instructions that come with them, for the time required by the longest cooking grain in the mixture.

Cooked rice may be cooked in bulk and frozen for several weeks, sealed in airtight plastic bags. This is particularly useful if you want brown rice at short notice.

CRUSTY RICE CAKES

These delicious little cakes are particularly good made with brown rice but may be made with any cooked rice.

To cook short or long-grain brown rice, allow 3 cups of water and 1/2–1 teaspoon of salt to each cup of rice, and simmer for 45 minutes to an hour in a pot with the lid ajar. If the pot seems dry before the rice is tender, add more water. If tender before all water is absorbed, drain off excess water. This makes 2–3 cups of cooked brown rice. Refrigerate for up to 3 days, or freeze for up to a month.

For 2–3 servings, put in a bowl 1½ cups cooked brown rice, 1 large egg, 2–3 tablespoons grated parmesan cheese and 2 tablespoons basil pesto. Mix with a fork until combined, then drop in spoonfuls into a hot, non-stick frying pan containing a little canola or other oil.

Cook over moderate heat for about 10 minutes per side until golden brown and crunchy. Serve with any main dish which does not contain grain.

BULGAR (OR BURGHUL)

This is a quickly prepared grain made from chopped wheat which has been pre-cooked and dried. It may be used in place of rice, by itself, or in mixtures. (It is not the same as kibbled wheat, which is chopped wheat that has not been pre-cooked and has a raw flavour if prepared as burghul is.)

1 cup of burghul absorbs 1–1½ cups of liquid. Either pour boiling vegetable stock over it and leave to stand for 10–15 minutes, or bring the bulgar and stock to the boil, remove from the heat and leave to stand for 5–10 minutes, until the liquid is absorbed. Add herbs, or other seasonings if desired. Serve in place of plain cooked rice, or leave to get cold and add vegetables and dressing to make a salad.

KIBBLED WHEAT AND KIBBLED MIXED GRAINS

Kibbled grains are chopped but not pre-cooked. They cook much more quickly than the whole, unchopped grains, but take longer than bulgar.

Heat 1 cup of kibbled wheat or mixed grains in 1 tablespoon of oil over moderate heat, for 4–5 minutes. Add 2 cups vegetable stock or 2 cups water with 2 teaspoons of vegetable stock powder and cook gently, with the lid ajar for 20–30 minutes. If the liquid is absorbed before the grains are as tender as you like, add more water and simmer for longer.

PASTA

As with rice, there is now a wide variety of fresh and dried pasta available in most supermarkets. As if this is not enough, various types of Asian noodles have also appeared on the shelves.

When buying pasta, look for the varieties that are made from 100% durum wheat, as these have a firmer texture when cooked.

This book contains a number of recipes for main meal pasta and noodle dishes (pages 64–73); while almost any of these could be served in smaller quantities as side dishes, 'plain' lightly oiled or buttered pasta and noodles make great 'sides'. (For a slightly more elaborate 'side' toss cooked pasta with a little olive oil, 1–2 tablespoons of your favourite pesto and a little grated parmesan cheese.)

For best results all pasta (fresh or dried) should be cooked in plenty of rapidly boiling water. Cooking times can vary quite widely, depending on the size or shape of the pasta, so check the instructions on the pack. Asian noodles (except for rice sticks or noodles) should generally be cooked the same way although cooking times often seem to be shorter. Rice sticks/noodles don't actually require 'cooking', just a 5–10 minute soak in boiling water.

POTATOES

Potatoes are a useful basic ingredient and may be used in many ways, as part of a main course dish, in salads (especially in warm weather) and as side dishes, especially when baked.

Choose waxy, firm potatoes for salads and for slicing into quiches, frittata, vegetable squares, etc., and floury potatoes for mashing and baking.

EASY PRE-COOKED POTATOES

The easiest and fastest way we know to pre-cook potatoes is to slice or cube them (depending on the way you want them cut, when they are cooked) and to microwave them in an oven bag, a tough plastic bag or a small dish which they almost fill. Add a tablespoon of water per potato, close the container or bag, leaving a little space for steam to escape, and microwave, allowing about 2–3 minute per 100g of potato. Cook for a little longer if potatoes are not quite ready. Drain if necessary, cool and use as desired. For mashed potatoes, simply squeeze the bag containing the cooked potatoes, then transfer to a bowl and beat with a fork, adding a little salt, milk, and butter if desired.

SAUTÉED POTATOES

Leftover boiled or microwaved potatoes may be sliced or cubed, and fried in a little olive oil in a non-stick frying pan for 15–20 minutes, turning once or twice, until they are golden brown and crusty. These make a very popular 'side'.

MICROWAVE-BAKED POTATOES

Scrub potatoes and pierce each one quite deeply, in several places. Place potatoes in a circle, the same distance from the centre of the oven. Cook on full power, allowing about 5½ minutes for 200g, 7–8 minutes for 300g and 10 minutes for 400g. Turn upside down, about halfway through, and leave to stand for a few minutes after cooking. When serving a baked potato as a 'side', cut a cross in its top, squeeze the sides between the cuts so the cross opens up, and add cottage or cream cheese, butter, or a little of your favourite pesto. A piece of your favourite cheese makes a tasty topping, too.

CONVENIENT COUSCOUS

Couscous is a busy cook's dream come true – invaluable for anyone who wants food on the table fast!

A relative newcomer to supermarket shelves (and often available loose, in bulk foods departments), it has a widely popular texture and flavour. It is a good accompaniment when cooked plainly but, since it can be flavoured in many ways, it appeals to cooks who like to experiment with different seasonings. The quick-cooking couscous we buy is, in fact, pin-head sized pellets of pre-cooked pasta.

For 4 people, put 1 cup of couscous in a bowl and add 2 teaspoons of butter or 1 teaspoon each of your favourite pesto and olive oil. Add 2 teaspoons vegetable stock powder then stir in 2 cups of boiling water (or replace stock powder and water with boiling stock). Cover and leave to stand for 5–6 minutes. At the end of this time, all the liquid will be absorbed. Check seasonings and serve, or stir in pepper, any pre-cooked flavourings you like, and chopped parsley or herbs.

When serving couscous with a 'saucy' dish alongside, you can add 1$\frac{1}{2}$ instead of 2 cups of water, so it soaks up sauce on the plate.

(For main course couscous recipes, see page 62.)

PERSIAN COUSCOUS

Colourful and tasty, with interesting textures, this makes an interesting side or even main dish.

FOR 2–4 SERVINGS:

1 cup couscous
2 teaspoons vegetable stock powder
$\frac{1}{2}$ teaspoon sugar
grated rind of $\frac{1}{2}$ an orange, optional
2 cups boiling water
$\frac{1}{4}$–$\frac{1}{2}$ cup chopped almonds or pine nuts
$\frac{1}{4}$–$\frac{1}{2}$ cup currants
2 tablespoons butter or olive oil
$\frac{1}{4}$–$\frac{1}{2}$ cup dried apricots
2 spring onions
$\frac{1}{4}$ cup chopped coriander leaves, if available

Stir the couscous, stock powder, sugar and grated orange rind together in a bowl. Add the boiling water, cover and leave to stand for 6 minutes.

Heat the nuts and currants in the butter or oil in a small frying pan, over moderate heat, until the nuts brown lightly and the currants puff up. Chop and add the apricots.

Stir the hot nuts and fruit through the couscous. Serve hot, warm or at room temperature, adding the finely chopped spring onions and coriander just before serving.

VERY EASY VEGETARIAN

THE MAIN EVENT

What will we eat tonight?

Our 'Mains' section, the biggest in this book, is intended to answer this question, although you may get other easy ideas from different parts of this book too, especially from the soup section.

In an effort to make your life easier and your cooking simpler (and leave you with fewer dishes to wash) we have often put several different main ingredients in one recipe, taking for granted that you will want to make only one composite dish most nights, perhaps serving it with bread and a simple salad.

There will be some times, however, when you want to make a couple of dishes. Maybe you want to please people with different tastes, are catering for particularly hungry people, or would like to give your friends and family a choice. In this case, look through the mains, soups, salads and finger foods sections before making your second choice.

Our composite recipes have made it rather difficult for us to divide our 'Mains' neatly into subsections. Take 'eggs' for example. We have grouped several egg dishes together, but you will find a number of other recipes containing two, three or four eggs in our pies and vegetable dishes. You won't even find a heading for 'Cheesy Mains', because we have used cheese with pasta, vegetables, and so on, and listed our cheese recipes under these headings.

Last but not least, as you make and eat the dishes we have listed here, we hope you will keep a pencil handy! Forget that your mother taught you not to write on books, and make your own personal notes about serving sizes, cooking times, and popularity ratings. Then, the next time you try a recipe, you will find it even quicker and easier. Although this applies to all the recipes, it seems most important in the 'Mains' section. Enjoy!

Pumpkin and Mushroom Risotto

PUMPKIN AND MUSHROOM RISOTTO

Pumpkin gives this risotto a warm autumnal glow, and a slightly sweet flavour with a deliciously earthy note provided by the mushrooms. We have used Italian arborio rice, but Australian calrose rice also works very well in risottos.

FOR 3–4 LARGE SERVINGS:

1 medium-sized onion
2 tablespoons olive or canola oil
1 teaspoon (1–2 cloves) minced garlic
250g seeded and peeled pumpkin
250g brown button mushrooms
1 tablespoon olive or canola oil
1 cup arborio (or calrose) rice
$2^{1}/_{2}$–3 cups hot water or mushroom stock
1 tablespoon basil pesto
2–3 tablespoons grated parmesan cheese
$^{1}/_{2}$–1 cup fresh or frozen peas
$^{1}/_{2}$–1 teaspoon salt
black pepper to taste

Peel, quarter and slice the onion while the oil heats in a large, preferably non-stick, frying pan. Add the onion and garlic then cook for 2–3 minutes until the onion has softened. Grate the pumpkin and halve the mushrooms, then add these and continue to cook, stirring frequently to avoid browning, for about 5 minutes. Remove the vegetable mixture from the pan and set aside.

Heat the second measure of oil in the pan, then stir in the rice and cook for 1–2 minutes. Add the vegetable mixture and stir gently, then pour in 1 cup of the water or stock. Bring to the boil, then reduce the heat and leave the uncovered pan to simmer gently, stirring occasionally, until most of the liquid has disappeared (this should take about 3–4 minutes). Add another cup of liquid and when this liquid too has been absorbed (in another 4–5 minutes), add another $^{1}/_{2}$ cup of liquid and leave to simmer again.

When this liquid has almost gone, begin testing the rice. Test the rice for 'doneness' frequently once you have added the last of the water (if the liquid has all gone before the rice is cooked, gradually add an extra half cup or so). Take care not to overcook or the rice will turn mushy, but do not serve undercooked either – hard-centred rice is very unpleasant!

As soon as the grains are tender right through, add the pesto, parmesan cheese and peas then cook, stirring frequently, until the peas are cooked, another 3–4 minutes. Season with salt and pepper to taste and serve immediately. (You may not need any salt if you used stock powder.)

SPICED RICE SCRAMBLE

Put together this delicious and unusual rice recipe for a main meal, and serve leftovers cold as a salad. The final assembly takes next to no time, but you must do a little preparation ahead.

FOR 4 SERVINGS:

PREPARE AHEAD:
4 cups cooked basmati rice ($1^{1}/_{2}$ cups raw)
1 teaspoon salt
1 cup Californian raisins
3 tablespoons balsamic or wine vinegar
3 tablespoons water
1 each red and yellow peppers, if available

SAUCE:
2 tablespoons each tomato paste, water and sherry
1 tablespoon each sesame oil, oyster or Hoisin sauce and Thai sweet chilli sauce

4 eggs
3 tablespoons water or milk
$^{1}/_{4}$ teaspoon salt
1 tablespoon butter or oil
1 tablespoon oil
$^{1}/_{4}$–$^{1}/_{2}$ cup pine nuts
4 spring onions, finely chopped

Prepare the rice, raisins, peppers, and sauce before you need them, up to several hours ahead.

Microwave the rice in a large covered bowl with $3^{1}/_{2}$ cups of boiling water and the salt for about 20 minutes. Leave to stand for at least 10 minutes until all the water is absorbed.

Boil the raisins in the vinegar and water in a small pot or frying pan for 5–10 minutes, until all the liquid has disappeared.

If using peppers, turn them under a grill for 5 minutes or until their skins have charred on all sides. Cool in a plastic bag, peel off skin and chop flesh in small pieces.

Make the sauce by shaking together the sauce ingredients in a screw-topped jar.

About 10 minutes before serving, assemble the dish.

With a fork, beat the eggs with the water or milk and the second measure of salt. Heat a large non-stick frying pan and scramble the eggs in 1 tablespoon of butter or oil until they are set, then remove from pan.

In the second tablespoon of oil in the same pan, lightly brown the pine nuts, then add the raisins and heat through. Tip in the rice and toss over fairly high heat until hot, then fold in the prepared peppers, eggs and spring onions and heat through.

Add the sauce, toss everything together, and serve alone or with tomatoes.

Spiced Rice Scramble

SPICY MUSHROOM PILAU

This may sound like an unusual combination of flavours, but it really is delicious! Despite a fairly long ingredients list, everything is cooked in one pan and it is really very simple.

FOR 3–4 SERVINGS:

$1\frac{1}{2}$ cups basmati rice
2 tablespoons canola oil
1 medium-large onion
1 teaspoon (1–2 cloves) minced garlic
1–2 teaspoons minced ginger
5cm piece cinnamon stick
6 whole cloves
2 cardamom pods, crushed
2 bay leaves
$\frac{1}{2}$ teaspoon each mustard seeds and black pepper corns
$\frac{1}{2}$–1 teaspoon minced red chilli or chilli powder, optional
250g mushrooms, sliced
$\frac{1}{2}$ red pepper, diced, optional
2 cups hot mushroom stock or 2 teaspoons mushroom stock powder and 2 cups hot water
$\frac{1}{2}$–1 teaspoon salt
2–3 tablespoons chopped fresh coriander leaf

Measure the rice into a large bowl, cover with cold water and leave to stand for 5–10 minutes.

Heat the oil in a large, preferably lidded, non-stick frying pan, and while it heats peel and dice the onion. Add the onion, garlic, ginger, whole spices and the chilli (if using) and cook, stirring frequently until the onion is soft and is turning clear.

Slice the mushrooms and deseed and dice the red pepper (if using). Drain and rinse the rice, then add it to the pan along with the mushrooms and pepper. Add the stock and stir until evenly mixed.

Allow the mixture to come to the boil, then reduce the heat to a very gentle simmer. Cover the pan with a close-fitting lid and cook for 10–15 minutes, stirring every few minutes to prevent sticking, until the rice is tender.

Season to taste with salt, then stir in the fresh coriander and serve.

SEASONAL SPECIALS:
Make the most of seasonal and supermarket specials of mushrooms, asparagus and avocados. Two grilled flat brown mushrooms, half a dozen lightly cooked asparagus stalks or a sliced avocado put in split french bread or ciabatta with a couple of slices of brie or camembert make a delicious, almost instant gourmet meal.

ASPARAGUS RISOTTO

Celebrate the start of spring with this tasty risotto! Buy Italian arborio rice which is traditionally used to make risotto, or the cheaper calrose rice which we find does a good job, too.

FOR 2–3 SERVINGS:

about 250g (10 medium-sized stalks) asparagus
2 cups vegetable stock or 2 teaspoons vegetable stock powder and 2 cups water
2 tablespoons butter
1 medium-sized onion, finely chopped
1 teaspoon (1–2 cloves) minced garlic
1 cup calrose or arborio rice
$\frac{1}{4}$ cup dry white wine or extra stock
salt and pepper
$\frac{1}{2}$ cup grated tasty cheddar cheese
grated parmesan cheese to serve

Cut the asparagus stalks diagonally into 4cm pieces. Put them (with any trimmings and stalk bottoms, etc.) into a medium-sized pot with the vegetable stock, cover, and boil for 3–4 minutes until barely tender. Drain, reserving the cooking liquid in another container, discard trimmings, and put aside the asparagus.

In the same pot or a medium-sized non-stick frying pan melt the butter, add the onion and garlic and cook over moderate heat for 3–4 minutes until onion is transparent but not brown. Add the rice, mix thoroughly, and cook for about a minute, stirring frequently.

Add the wine to the reserved stock, if you are using it. Add $\frac{1}{4}$ cup of stock to the rice, then add more, in $\frac{1}{4}$ cup lots each few minutes, or as the rice soaks it up and seems dry. Stir at regular intervals, since stirring helps to make the mixture creamy, and between stirrings cover with a lid.

The rice should be tender after 20 minutes, with no uncooked core in the middle of each grain. If not, add $\frac{1}{4}$ cup of water and cook longer. Stir in the asparagus and heat over very low heat for about 5 minutes.

At the end of this time, half an hour after you started cooking the onion, the rice grains should be soft and clumping together, with no liquid left. Add enough salt and pepper to bring out the asparagus flavour, then fold the grated tasty cheese through the risotto. Sprinkle with parmesan cheese and serve straight away.

Serve alone or with a salad and warmed bread rolls.

Asparagus Risotto

TRICOLOUR BULGAR PILAF

This pilaf is easy and relatively quick to prepare. Served with a salad it makes an interesting light meal, or alternatively it can be served in smaller quantities as a side dish.

FOR 3 LARGE OR 6 SIDE SERVINGS:

1 medium-sized red onion
1 tablespoon olive or canola oil
2–3 tablespoons (25g) butter or margarine
1 teaspoon (1–2 cloves) minced garlic
1 teaspoon minced red chilli or chilli powder, optional
1 each red, yellow and green pepper
1$\frac{1}{2}$ cups bulgar wheat
1$\frac{1}{2}$–2 cups hot water or vegetable stock
2–3 tablespoons chopped fresh herbs (coriander and/or parsley)
salt and pepper to taste

Dice the onion then heat the oil in a large, lidded frying pan. Add and melt the butter or margarine then stir in the onion, garlic and chilli (if using) and cook until the onion has softened.

While the onion cooks, halve and deseed the peppers, then cut them into 1cm slices. Add these to the pan and sauté for 2–3 minutes before adding the bulgar. Cook for 1–2 minutes, stirring the mixture so that all the grain is coated with oil, before adding 1$\frac{1}{2}$ cups of water or stock. Bring to the boil, then reduce the heat to a gentle simmer and cover the pan. Simmer gently for 10–15 minutes, stirring occasionally, until the liquid has been soaked up and the grain is tender. If all the liquid is absorbed too soon (before the bulgar is tender), add some or all of the remaining water or stock.

Once the grain is cooked, stir in the chopped fresh herbs, season with salt and pepper and serve.

RICE:
Some rice can be used and cooked interchangeably in the same ways, while others need different treatment.

Short-grain rices absorb a lot of water during cooking and tend to be slightly sticky when cooked. This is useful (and desirable) in some circumstances, such as sushi and puddings, but not in others.

Medium-grain rice absorbs less water than short-grain rice, so grains are soft but more separate when cooked. Calrose and arborio rice fall into this category.

Long-grain rices are light, fluffy and quite dry when cooked properly. They are widely used, and are often served under saucy foods.

SPINACH AND RICE CAKE

In this recipe spinach, rice and eggs are baked together to form a substantial 'cake'. This is delicious cut into wedges and served hot, warm or cold.

FOR 4 SERVINGS:

1 cup rice, brown or white
1 medium-sized onion
1 tablespoon canola oil
250g frozen spinach, thawed and squeezed
$\frac{1}{2}$ teaspoon each basil and marjoram
1 teaspoon salt
black pepper to taste
1 cup (250g) cottage cheese
$\frac{1}{4}$ cup grated parmesan cheese
3 large eggs
2–3 tomatoes, thinly sliced

Bring a large pot of water to the boil and add the rice. Boil until the rice is just tender, 8–10 minutes for white rice or 12–15 minutes for brown rice, then drain.

While the rice cooks, dice the onion and heat the oil in a medium-sized frying pan. Add the onion and cook until it is soft and clear. Add the thawed, squeezed spinach and the seasonings, cook for 1–2 minutes longer, then remove from the heat.

Transfer the spinach and onion mixture to a large bowl, add the drained rice, cottage cheese, parmesan cheese and eggs, then mix thoroughly.

Non-stick spray or oil a 22–25cm round cake tin and spoon in the rice mixture, smoothing off the top. Arrange a layer of sliced tomatoes over the surface and bake at 180°C for 40 minutes.

Serve with bread and a salad, or cooked seasonal vegetables.

Fragrant rices such as basmati or jasmine have a unique flavour, but can be used in the same way as other long-grain rices and are ideal accompaniments for ethnic dishes.

Brown rice is less 'refined' and retains its outer husks. The husks add nutritive value and stop cooked grains sticking together. Most white rice varieties can also be obtained in brown forms. Unfortunately, brown rice takes about twice as long to cook as white, however, it can be frozen after cooking, when speed is important.

Par-boiled rice has a yellowish appearance and grains stick together less than 'normal' white rice when cooked.

Rice mixtures look attractive, but often take as long as brown rice to cook.

Tricolour Bulgar Pilaf

CREAMY HERBED POLENTA WITH ROASTED WINTER VEGETABLES

Polenta (grainy yellow corn meal) is satisfyingly 'rib sticking' on a cold winter's night, especially when you team it with your favourite roasted winter vegetables and gravy! Although Cheesy Polenta is fine with this combination, here's another possibility, flavoured with herbs and cheese.

FOR 2–3 SERVINGS:

1 tablespoon butter
1 teaspoon (1–2 cloves) minced garlic
1 cup quick-cooking or plain polenta
about 3 cups vegetable stock or 3 teaspoons vegetable stock
    powder and 3 cups water
1 tablespoon basil, rocket or coriander pesto
$\frac{1}{4}$ cup finely chopped parsley or other fresh herbs
about $\frac{1}{4}$ cup sour cream or fresh cream
salt and pepper to taste

Heat the butter and garlic in a non-stick frying pan until it bubbles, then add the polenta and 2 cups of stock. Stir until smooth then cover and simmer for 5–10 minutes. Add more stock until it is like sloppy mashed potatoes, cover and simmer for 5 minutes more for quick-cooking polenta or 10 minutes more for regular polenta. Add extra stock or water if it gets thicker than creamy mashed potatoes.

Beat in the pesto, fresh herbs and cream, season to taste, then serve piled in a bowl or on a plate, with roasted vegetables and gravy (see page 88).

ROASTED WINTER VEGETABLES

Use the amounts of several vegetables that suit you. Scrub or thinly peel kumara, pumpkin, potatoes, and parsnip, and cut in even slices 1cm thick. Cut unpeeled zucchini in 1cm diagonal slices. Trim stems of large flat mushrooms level with the gills. Cut white or red onions in 1cm thick rings, or in quarters or sixths lengthwise.

Brush vegetables with olive oil. Cook in a double-sided contact grill (see page 8) heated to medium, for 10–15 minutes, or roast at 200°C in a cast iron baking dish or heavy roasting pan for 20–30 minutes, turning halfway through. Test grilled or roasted vegetables at regular intervals, removing those which cook first earlier, when they are tender and attractively browned. Brush with a little pesto diluted with oil in the last few minutes of cooking, if you like.

CHEESY POLENTA WITH ROASTED SUMMER VEGETABLES

Alison makes this meal in 15–20 minutes, 'roasting' vegetables for two in her double-sided contact grill (see page 8) and simmering quick-cooking polenta in less than 10 minutes. If you haven't used it before, polenta is like slightly grainy mashed potato – good 'comfort food'.

FOR 2–3 SERVINGS:

1 tablespoon olive oil or butter
1 teaspoon (1–2 cloves) minced garlic
$\frac{1}{4}$–$\frac{1}{2}$ teaspoon minced red chilli or chilli powder, optional
1 cup quick-cooking or regular polenta
about 3 cups vegetable stock or 3 teaspoons vegetable stock
    powder and 3 cups water
3 tablespoons grated parmesan cheese
salt and pepper to taste

Heat the butter or oil, garlic and chilli (if using) in a medium-sized non-stick frying pan until it bubbles, then add the polenta (grainy yellow corn meal) and 2 cups of the stock. Stir until smooth, then cover and simmer for about 5 minutes. Add more stock until it is like very sloppy mashed potato, then cover and cook for about 5 minutes for quick-cooking polenta or 10 minutes for regular polenta. Add extra stock or water to reach mashed potato consistency.

At the end of this time beat in the parmesan cheese and enough salt and pepper to bring out its mild, pleasant flavour. (For extra flavour, stir in sun-dried tomato or basil pesto or tapenade.) When vegetables are cooked, pile the polenta on plates or bowls and top with the roasted vegetables.

ROASTED SUMMER VEGETABLES

Use amounts and types of vegetable to suit yourself. Quarter peppers of several colours, removing seeds and pith, cut the stems of mushrooms level with their caps, cut eggplant in 1cm slices, zucchini in 1cm diagonal slices, and small red onions into quarters lengthways.

Brush vegetables on both sides with olive oil, plain or flavoured with a crushed, sliced garlic clove. Cook in a double-sided contact grill (see page 8) preheated to Medium, for about 5 minutes, or cook under a regular grill, turning after half time, for 10–15 minutes, or roast uncovered at 200°C for 20–30 minutes, taking out mushrooms before other vegetables if necessary. Brush with olive oil mixed with your favourite pesto, or with Tex-Mex Dressing (see page 43) just before serving.

Cheesy Polenta with Roasted Summer Vegetables

NEARLY NIÇOISE COUSCOUS

This 'warm weather' recipe is easy enough for an after-work meal and colourful enough for friends. It can be made, start to finish, in about 15 minutes, or prepared before work and assembled at the last minute.

FOR 2–3 SERVINGS:

4 eggs
1 cup couscous
2 teaspoons basil pesto, optional
2 teaspoons vegetable stock powder
1½ cups boiling water
about 10 green beans
3–4 large tomatoes

2 tablespoons chopped parsley, flat-leafed if possible
2 tablespoons chopped coriander leaves
8–12 black olives
lemon wedges, optional

DRESSING:
1–2 cloves garlic, minced
¼ teaspoon salt
1 teaspoon basil pesto, optional
2 tablespoons lemon juice
3–4 tablespoons olive oil

Cover the eggs with hot water, bring to the boil and simmer for 10 minutes, then cool immediately in cold water, shelling when cool enough to handle.

Put the couscous in a fairly large bowl with the pesto and stock powder, pour over the boiling water, stir to mix then cover and leave to stand for at least 6 minutes.

Slice the beans diagonally in 3cm lengths and cook in a little water for 2–3 minutes (or put in with the eggs after 7 or 8 minutes) then drain. Cut the tomatoes into 1cm cubes.

Shake the dressing ingredients together in a screw-topped jar.

Just before serving, fork through the couscous, then fold in most of the beans, tomatoes and chopped herbs. Transfer to a serving dish or individual plates or bowls, and top with the quartered hard-boiled eggs, remaining beans, tomatoes and herbs, and the olives. Drizzle with the dressing and serve with lemon wedges if desired.

This is good served warm, if you have just made it, or at room temperature, rather than very cold, straight from the refrigerator.

NOTE: For semi-vegetarians, add some chopped anchovies.

SPICY ROASTED VEGETABLES WITH COUSCOUS

Roasted vegetables, chickpeas and couscous combine in this interesting combination of colours, flavours and textures. The ingredients list may seem long but most are simply used in a marinade for the vegetables.

FOR 3–4 LARGE SERVINGS:

3 tablespoons olive or canola oil
2 tablespoons lemon juice
1 tablespoon dark soy sauce
1 teaspoon (1–2 cloves) minced garlic
1½ teaspoons each ground cumin and coriander
½ teaspoon sugar
¼ teaspoon minced red chilli or chilli powder
¼ teaspoon ground cloves
2 peppers (red, yellow, green or a combination)
2 medium-sized zucchini
2 medium-sized carrots
1 medium-sized red onion
1 cup couscous
310g can chickpeas
1 cup boiling water or vegetable stock
1–2 tablespoons chopped flat-leafed parsley or mint
salt and pepper to taste

Measure the first nine ingredients into a screw-topped jar and shake to combine for the marinade.

Halve and deseed the peppers, then cut the flesh into strips 1–2cm wide. Slice the zucchini and carrots lengthways into strips or ribbons 0.5–1cm thick and cut the onion into eight thin wedges.

Put the prepared vegetables in a plastic bag with the marinade and toss everything together so the vegetables are evenly coated with the marinade. Leave the vegetables to marinate for 5–10 minutes, then tip them into a shallow roasting pan (or sponge roll tin) and bake/roast them for 12–15 minutes at 225°C. Alternatively, cook the vegetables until tender in a double-sided contact grill (see page 8) on medium for about 5 minutes.

While the vegetables cook, measure the couscous into a large bowl. Add the chickpeas then the boiling water or stock. Leave to stand for 5 minutes then fluff with a fork. Cut the cooked vegetables into 1–2cm pieces, then stir these into the couscous mixture along with any remaining marinade or cooking juices. Toss the mixture together, adding salt, pepper and chopped herbs to taste, before serving.

Nearly Niçoise Couscous

RAVIOLI IN WALNUT CREAM SAUCE

Most supermarkets now stock different types of filled pasta suitable for vegetarians. Coupled with a simple sauce, any of these can make a great, quickly prepared meal.

FOR 2–3 LARGE OR 4–5 STARTER SERVINGS:

300g 'vegetarian' filled ravioli, tortellini, etc.
1/2 cup walnut pieces
1 cup (50g) lightly packed basil leaves
1/2–3/4 cup cream
1/4 cup grated parmesan cheese
1/2 teaspoon salt
black pepper to taste
2 tablespoons butter
extra grated parmesan and/or chopped fresh basil

Bring a large pot of water to the boil then put the pasta in to cook. While the pasta cooks, prepare the sauce.

Place the walnut pieces in a blender or food processor, and process until finely chopped, then add the basil leaves and process again. Pour in 1/2 cup of cream and add the parmesan cheese, salt and pepper. Process until you have a fairly smooth sauce that is just pourable (add the extra cream if it's too thick).

Drain the cooked pasta, then return it to the cooking pot with the butter and the sauce. Return the pot to the warm (but switched off) element and stir very gently until the butter is melted and the pasta is coated with the sauce.

Serve immediately, topped with a little extra grated parmesan and/or chopped fresh basil.

TOMATO AND OLIVE PESTO

What could be easier to prepare (or more delicious!) than pasta with this simple uncooked tomato and olive sauce.

FOR 2–3 SERVINGS;

200g pasta, long or short
3 medium-sized tomatoes
2 cloves garlic
1/2 cup blanched or slivered almonds
1/2 cup lightly packed basil leaves
3 tablespoons olive oil
1/4 cup pitted black olives
salt and pepper to taste

Bring a large pot of water to the boil, then add the pasta. While the pasta cooks, prepare the pesto.

Halve the tomatoes, then scoop out and discard the seeds and roughly chop the flesh. Put the tomato flesh, garlic, almonds, basil and oil in a food processor, and blend until smooth. Add the olives and salt and pepper to taste ,then process briefly so some chunks of olive remain.

Drain the cooked pasta, toss in the sauce, serve and enjoy!

PASTA WITH SUMMER SAUCE

A cold, uncooked sauce stirred through hot pasta makes an easy and nutritious meal on a hot day. Don't be put off by the long ingredients list – it is becuase of the seasonings, which are important for a good flavour.

FOR 2–3 SERVINGS:

150–200g large spiral pasta
1 large avocado
4 ripe red (preferably Italian) tomatoes (about 400g)
1/4–1/2 red onion
1 teaspoon (1–2 cloves) minced garlic
8 large basil leaves
2 teaspoons capers
3–4 tablespoons extra virgin olive oil
2 teaspoons balsamic vinegar
2 teaspoons lime juice
1/2 teaspoon sugar
1/2–1 teaspoon salt
1/4 teaspoon minced red chilli or chilli powder
1/2 teaspoon dried oreganum, crumbled
black pepper to taste
2–3 tablespoons grated parmesan cheese

Cook the pasta in plenty of boiling, lightly salted water with about 1 tablespoon of oil or butter added. Drain when cooked.

While pasta is cooking, cut the avocado and tomatoes into 1cm cubes and put in a bowl. Add the finely chopped onion, garlic, roughly chopped basil and capers.

Mix the remaining ingredients thoroughly, and toss through the vegetable mixture.

When ready to serve, put the hot drained pasta into a shallow bowl, toss half the sauce through it, and spoon the rest over the top. Serve at once.

VARIATIONS: Add any of the following: 6–8 black olives, 4 chopped sun-dried tomatoes, 50g cubed feta cheese, 1/2 cup toasted pine nuts, chopped parsley.

If you are semi-vegetarian, reduce the salt and add several finely chopped anchovies to the dressing.

Pasta with Summer Sauce

BAKED MACARONI CHEESE AND VEGETABLES

Macaroni cheese is a perennial favourite – this variation has vegetables included, making it a more-or-less complete meal.

FOR 4 LARGE SERVINGS:

250g pasta, macaroni, torroncini (in photo), spirals, etc.
200g broccoli, cut into small florets
400g can whole tomatoes in juice
25g butter
3 tablespoons flour
1 cup milk
1/2–1 teaspoon salt
black pepper to taste
1 tablespoon basil pesto
1 cup grated tasty cheese
1/4 cup pumpkin seeds

Turn the oven on to preheat to 225°C. Bring a large pot of water to the boil, then add the pasta. When the pasta is almost cooked (see packet instructions, but usually after about 8–10 minutes boiling) add the broccoli florets and cook for a further 2–3 minutes. When the pasta is cooked, drain the pasta-broccoli mixture then transfer it to a lightly oiled or non-stick sprayed 25 x 30cm casserole dish.

Drain the tomatoes, reserving the juice, and roughly chop the flesh, then add this to the pasta mixture. Melt the butter in the pot you used to cook the pasta, stir in the flour and cook, stirring continuously, for about a minute. Add half the milk and stir until the mixture thickens and boils, ensuring there are no lumps. Add the remaining milk and the reserved tomato juice, allow the sauce to thicken and boil again. Remove the sauce from the heat then add salt and pepper to taste, basil pesto and grated cheese. Stir until the cheese has melted.

Pour the sauce over the pasta and vegetable mixture, and stir to combine. Sprinkle with the pumpkin seeds, then bake at 225°C for 10–15 minutes or until the top begins to brown.

Serve alone or with a salad and/or crusty bread.

EGG AND CHEESE PASTA BAKE

Even easier than conventional macaroni cheese, this dish is bound to become part of many cooks' repertoires. You can make it with 'ordinary' cheddar cheese but, for something really special, try a more exotic cheese such as gruyère, emmentaler or even raclette.

FOR 2–3 LARGE SERVINGS:

250g dried pasta (curls, spirals, route etc.)
1 tablespoon olive oil
1 medium-sized onion, peeled and diced
1 teaspoon (1–2 cloves) minced garlic
2 large eggs
1 cup cream
1 1/2–2 cups (150–200g) grated cheese, (cheddar, gruyère, emmentaler or raclette)

Turn the oven on to preheat to 200°C then put the pasta on to cook in plenty of boiling water. While the pasta cooks, heat the oil in a large frying pan then add the onion and garlic and sauté until the onion has softened and turned clear. Remove the pan from the heat and set aside. Whisk together the eggs and cream.

Drain the cooked pasta well, then transfer back to the cooking pot. Stir in the onion-garlic mixture, the egg mixture and about half of the grated cheese. Tip the pasta mixture into a lightly oiled or non-stick sprayed 20 x 25cm casserole dish and sprinkle with the remaining grated cheese.

Bake at 200°C for 20–25 minutes until the edges are bubbling and the top has browned (if the top has not browned after this time turn the oven to grill for a few minutes).

PASTA:
There are many, many different shapes of pasta, with no hard-and-fast rules to govern their use. The most simple division is between long (spaghetti, fettuccine, etc.) and short (macaroni, penne, etc.) pasta but within these general types they can be used more-or-less interchangeably – don't be put off if you don't have the shape listed. Remember, the more convoluted the shape (the more fins, ridges, etc.) the more sauce the pasta will hold. Cook pasta in plenty of boiling water, following the packet instructions.

Baked Macaroni Cheese and Vegetables

PENNE WITH SPINACH AND BLUE CHEESE SAUCE

Pasta sauces don't get much simpler than this. The delicious creamy blue cheeses now available have a quite mild flavour and are excellent for sauces like this, providing just the right amount of 'blue-cheese' flavour.

FOR 2–3 LARGE SERVINGS:

250g short pasta (penne, macaroni, spirals, curls, etc.)
250g fresh spinach
125g creamy blue cheese
¼ cup milk
¼ teaspoon grated nutmeg
½ teaspoon salt
black pepper
2–3 tablespoons butter
½–1 cup grated cheese, optional

Put the pasta on to cook in plenty of boiling water. While the pasta cooks, wash the spinach in plenty of cold water. Remove any tough stems and separate the leaves then transfer the spinach to a large lidded frying pan or pot. Cook the spinach (using only the water clinging to the leaves) until the leaves and stems are wilted.

Crumble the blue cheese and combine it with the milk, nutmeg, salt and pepper in a small microwave dish or pot. Microwave on full power for about 2 minutes, or heat gently, stirring frequently, until the cheese has melted. Set aside until the pasta is cooked.

Drain the cooked pasta, then return it to the cooking pot and toss with the butter. Squeeze excess water from the cooked spinach, then add this and the sauce to the pasta. Stir gently to combine, and leave to stand for 2–3 minutes before serving, or transfer to a lightly oiled or non-stick sprayed 20 x 25cm casserole dish, sprinkle with grated cheese and brown the top under the grill.

Pesto must be one of the simplest (and most authentic) pasta sauces. Just stir plenty of your favourite pesto through lightly oiled pasta and top with a grind of black pepper and some shaved or grated parmesan to make a really simple main, or add 1–2 tablespoons of pesto (per 100g uncooked pasta) thinned with a little cream or olive oil to make an interesting side dish.

ROAST PUMPKIN RAVIOLI

Use wonton wrappers to make quick ravioli. Serve a few in a bowl as a starter course, or a pile in a bigger bowl for a main course for two, with crusty bread and side salads.

FOR 12 WONTONS:

24 wonton wrappers
1 medium-sized onion
400g peeled and deseeded pumpkin
1 tablespoon olive oil
2 teaspoons wine vinegar or balsamic vinegar
2 teaspoons sugar
100g feta cheese
2 cups vegetable stock

Thaw wonton wrappers if necessary.

Cut the peeled onion in half from top to bottom, then into eight wedges. Cut the prepared pumpkin into 2cm cubes.

Coat onion and pumpkin with the olive oil. Roast the onion and pumpkin at 200°C for about 30 minutes, until both are tender and lightly browned. Stir the vinegar and sugar through the vegetables after they have roasted for 20 minutes.

Mash the pumpkin and onion with the feta cheese. Taste and season if necessary, adding any fresh herb you like, and moistening with a little stock, milk or cream if necessary.

Place spoonfuls of the filling in the centre of 12 of the wonton wrappers. Place a sprig of fresh herb on the filling if desired. Brush around the filling with water to dampen, then top each 'filled' wonton with a plain wonton wrapper, pressing the tops and bottoms together carefully, without leaving any air bubbles. Leave the prepared ravioli square, or cut into rounds with a suitable cutter.

Simmer in a pot of vegetable stock for 5–6 minutes, until the ravioli are cooked. Serve immediately, in a little stock, with basil pesto.

VARIATION: Cut the onion and pumpkin in slices 1cm thick, brush with oil and cook for about 10 minutes on medium heat, in a double-sided contact grill (see page 8).

Roast Pumpkin Raviolli

MUSHROOM LASAGNE

Although it is simple, this lasagne will always be well received (at least by mushroom lovers)!

FOR 4–6 SERVINGS:

2 tablespoons olive or canola oil
1 large onion
2 teaspoons (2–3 cloves) minced garlic
500g mushrooms
1 tablespoon basil pesto
½ teaspoon salt
black pepper to taste
2–3 tablespoons butter
3 tablespoons flour
about ¼ teaspoon freshly grated nutmeg
½ teaspoon salt
2½ cups milk
1 cup grated tasty cheese
150–200g fresh lasagne sheets

Peel, quarter and slice the onion, then heat the oil in a large, preferably lidded, non-stick frying pan. Add the onion and garlic and cook, stirring frequently, until the onion is soft and clear. While the onion cooks, cut the mushrooms into 1cm slices, then gently stir them into the onion. Cover the pan and cook, stirring occasionally, until the mushrooms have softened and wilted. Remove from the heat and add the pesto, salt and pepper to taste.

Melt the butter in a medium-sized pot. Stir in the flour and cook, stirring continuously, for 1 minute. Add the nutmeg and salt then 1 cup of the milk. Stir well to ensure there are no lumps and allow the sauce to thicken and boil, then add the remaining milk and bring to the boil again, stirring frequently. Remove from the heat and stir in two-thirds of the grated cheese.

Lightly oil or non-stick spray a 20 x 25cm casserole dish. Spread half a cup of the cheese sauce over the bottom of the dish, then cover this with a sheet of lasagne. Cover this with half of the mushroom mixture, another half cup of cheese sauce, then another sheet of lasagne. Add the remaining mushroom mixture, half a cup of sauce and another sheet of lasagne.

Pour and spread the remaining cheese sauce over the top, sprinkle with the remaining cheese, then bake the lasagne for 30–40 minutes at 200°C, until the top is golden brown. Remove from the oven and leave to stand for 5 minutes before serving.

SPAGHETTI CARBONARA

This is a simple but quite delicious pasta sauce. The traditional version often includes matchsticks of ham, but it is delicious alone, with a handful of chopped fresh herbs or with any of the other additions suggested below.

FOR 4–6 SERVINGS:

400g fresh or dried spaghetti
2 eggs
½ cup cream
½ cup freshly grated parmesan cheese
½ teaspoon salt
25g (2–3 tablespoons) butter, cubed
black pepper to taste

Optional Extras:
¼ cup chopped fresh basil, parsley, chives, oreganum, etc.
¼–½ cup thinly sliced sun-dried tomatoes
½–1 cup lightly cooked baby peas
½–1 cup sautéed button mushrooms

Put the pasta on to cook in plenty of boiling water. While the pasta cooks, combine the eggs, cream, grated parmesan cheese and salt.

When the pasta is cooked, drain then return to the cooking pot and add the butter. As soon as the butter has melted, add the egg mixture and stir to thoroughly combine. The heat of the pasta and pot should thicken the sauce, making it thick and creamy. If the sauce is not thickening, return the pot to a very low heat (the switched off element will usually do) for a minute or two, stirring frequently.

Add a generous grind of black pepper and any one or two of the 'optional extras', then stir again and leave to stand for one minute. Serve immediately with extra grated parmesan and black pepper on hand.

STORING EGGS:
Eggs are so useful, you should make sure you always have some on hand. Buy eggs every few days, rather than keeping large numbers for a long time! Don't leave them sitting around in a hot car or in the sun, and put them in the refrigerator as soon as you get them home, since they stay fresher longer when kept cool.

Mushroom Lasagne

PEANUT DRESSED PASTA

This dish makes a quick and tasty main dish on its own, but is also particularly useful as part of a buffet. Serve it hot, or as a cool salad, as a main or side course, depending how your whim or the occasion dictates.

FOR 4 SERVINGS:

250–300g pasta or noodles (see note below)
1 medium-large carrot
2 medium-sized zucchini (or 200g broccoli or green beans)

DRESSING:
½ cup peanut butter
½ cup hot water
2 tablespoons each soy sauce, wine vinegar and brown sugar
1–2 teaspoons sesame oil
1 teaspoon minced ginger
½ teaspoon minced red chilli or chilli powder, optional
salt to taste
chopped spring onion or coriander leaf to garnish

Bring a large pot of water to the boil and put the pasta on to cook.

While the pasta cooks, prepare the vegetables by cutting the carrot and zucchini into long, thin (5–7mm) matchsticks (cut broccoli into small florets or slice beans lengthways). When the pasta is almost cooked, add the vegetables to the pot and cook for 1–2 minutes longer, until the pasta and vegetables are just cooked.

Combine the eight dressing ingredients in a screw-topped jar and shake until well combined, stirring to break up the peanut butter if required. Taste and add salt if required.

Drain the cooked pasta and vegetables well, then return them to the cooking pot or a serving bowl. Add the dressing and toss gently until well combined. Allow to stand for at least 2–3 minutes, then serve garnished with some chopped spring onions or coriander leaf.

NOTE: The style of this dish can be varied by the type of pasta or noodles you use. For an Asian-style dish use thin yellow egg noodles or Japanese soba noodles, or for a quite different style use 'conventional' pasta such as spaghetti or spirals.

SPICY RICE NOODLES

We love fried noodle dishes – this one combines some of our favourite flavours with the convenience of rice noodles (sometimes called rice sticks), which only require soaking, not cooking.

FOR 2–3 LARGE SERVINGS:

150g rice sticks or noodles
2 teaspoons oil
150g firm tofu, finely cubed
2 tablespoons dark soy sauce
1 tablespoon rice wine or sherry
1 teaspoon each minced ginger and sesame oil
1 teaspoon (1–2 cloves) minced garlic
½ teaspoon minced red chilli or chilli powder, optional
2 tablespoons canola oil
1 tablespoon red curry paste
1 medium-sized onion, peeled, quartered and sliced
1 large carrot, cut into matchsticks
150–200g broccoli florets
½ red pepper, sliced
½ green or yellow pepper, sliced
2 spring onions, cut into 2cm lengths
1–2 tablespoons extra oil and 1–2 tablespoons extra water, if required
1 cup mung or soy bean sprouts
2 tablespoons chopped coriander leaf, fresh or bottled
salt (or extra soy sauce) to taste

Place the rice sticks or noodles in a large pot or bowl and cover with boiling water. Leave to stand for 5–10 minutes (different brands take different times) or until tender, then drain and toss with about 2 teaspoons of oil.

Place the cubed tofu in a small bowl, add the next five ingredients plus the chilli if using, and stir to combine. Leave to stand while you prepare the remaining ingredients.

Heat the canola oil in a very large frying pan or wok, then add the red curry paste and the onion. Stir-fry until the onion begins to soften, then add the carrot and broccoli. Continue to stir-fry for about a minute, then add the peppers and the tofu mixture and cook for another 2–3 minutes.

Add the drained noodles and the spring onions, and stir-fry for 3–4 minutes, adding a little extra oil and/or water if the noodles are sticking. Toss in the bean sprouts and chopped coriander, add salt or additional soy sauce to taste, and stir to combine.

Serve immediately.

Spicy Rice Noodles

EASY VEGETABLE SQUARE

Make this useful recipe with canned, leftover cooked vegetables, or 'purpose cooked' vegetables. The pesto and parmesan cheese ensure a good, interesting flavour, even when mild-flavoured vegetables are used.

FOR 4 LARGE SERVINGS:

2–3 cups cooked drained vegetables
4 large eggs
3/4 cup low-fat or regular sour cream
6 tablespoons parmesan cheese
3 tablespoons basil pesto
3 tablespoons couscous or dry breadcrumbs
2 tomatoes, optional
about 1/2 cup grated cheddar cheese

Turn the oven on to 180°C to preheat.

Cook raw vegetables in a small amount of salted water until just tender, then drain thoroughly, in a sieve. OR use cooked leftover, or canned vegetables. (If vegetables are cooked without salt, add 1/2 teaspoon salt to the egg mixture.) Cut the cooked vegetables into pieces no bigger than 1cm cubes.

Put the eggs, sour cream, parmesan cheese and pesto in a bowl. Stir with a fork or whisk until well mixed.

Lightly butter or spray with non-stick spray a baking pan about 20cm square. Sprinkle the base with couscous or breadcrumbs, so any liquid which comes from the vegetables during baking will be soaked up. (If you have couscous, use it, because it works well and makes the base firmer, almost like a thin pastry crust.)

Sprinkle the well-drained cooked vegetables evenly over the base of the prepared pan, then pour the liquid over them. Shake gently so liquid surrounds the vegetables.

Cover the surface with slices of tomato (if you have them) then sprinkle with grated cheese. Bake at 180°C (on fan-bake if possible) for 30 minutes or until the top is golden brown and nicely risen, the sides are golden brown, and the centre feels firm. Leave for a few minutes before cutting into serving-sized pieces.

Suitable vegetables include asparagus, cabbage, cauliflower, young green beans, broccoli, whole kernel corn, kumara, squeezed spinach, well drained silver beet, young carrots, pumpkin, new potatoes, peas, frozen mixed vegetables, zucchini, mushrooms. Note: Tomatoes and eggplant are too wet to use for the main vegetable filling.

NELSON POTATOES AND EGGS

Apples and onions, browned together, have a wonderful flavour. Add potatoes for substance, and top the lot with an egg if you have one on hand, since the yolk makes a perfect sauce.

FOR 2–3 LARGE SERVINGS:

2 medium-sized onions (red if possible)
2 tablespoons butter or oil
3 medium-sized apples
3 large potatoes, sliced (600g)
1/2 cup liquid (apple juice, white wine or 1/2 teaspoon stock powder and 1/2 cup of water)
thyme or sage, optional
pepper and salt
2 or 3 poached eggs

Peel and halve the onions from top to bottom, then cut each half in 4–6 wedges. Cook in a large, lidded, non-stick frying pan in the butter or oil until transparent and browned on the edges. Raise the heat, add the peeled, sliced apples and cook uncovered, stirring often, until the apples are lightly browned, too.

Mix in the sliced potatoes, then add the liquid. Add a sprinkling of fresh or dried thyme or sage if you have them. Cover pan tightly and cook for about 20 minutes until potatoes are tender. Turn occasionally, adding extra liquid if the mixture becomes too dry before potatoes are cooked, or taking off the lid for a few minutes if mixture is too wet. Taste and adjust the seasonings.

If you would like a poached egg on top of each serving, cook these in another frying pan or pot when the potatoes are nearly cooked.

Pile the vegetable mixture on the plates, sit the poached eggs on top, add freshly ground pepper and chopped parsley, and serve immediately.

The yolk of a poached egg makes a natural sauce, coating the food underneath it deliciously. Try poached eggs on spinach, potatoes or asparagus. **To poach an egg**, bring 3–4 cm of water to the boil in a pan from which the egg can easily be lifted. Add 1 teaspoon of vinegar per egg and a little salt (these help set the egg white), gently break in the egg/s and cook for 3–4 minutes until the white closest to the yolk is as firm as you like it, then remove from the pan with a slotted fish slice. Serve immediately.

Easy Vegetable Square

CURRIED CAULIFLOWER AND EGGS

This is much more interesting and delicious than it sounds! Cooked this way, it may even be possible to slip cauliflower past its most vehement opponents. The eggs can be omitted for a vegan version.

FOR 3–4 LARGE SERVINGS:

4 eggs
1 medium-sized onion
2 medium-small potatoes (200g)
1 tablespoon canola oil
1 teaspoon each minced garlic and ginger
1 tablespoon curry powder
1 teaspoon garum masala
2 whole cardamom pods, crushed (optional)
4–5 whole cloves, optional
400g can whole tomatoes in juice
¾ cup coconut cream
250g cauliflower
½ cup frozen peas, optional
½ teaspoon salt
1–2 tablespoons chopped fresh or bottled coriander leaf

Put the eggs in a small pot and cover with hot water, bring to the boil and simmer for 12 minutes. (Making a small hole in the blunt end of each egg will help prevent them cracking or splitting.) Cover with cold water to cool, then peel and set them aside.

Peel and slice the onion and cut the potatoes into 1cm cubes. Heat the oil in a large frying pan, then add the onion, potatoes, garlic and ginger. Cook (preferably covered) without browning, for 5 minutes, stirring occasionally, then add the curry powder, garum masala, and cardamom and cloves (if using). Continue to cook, stirring frequently, for 1 minute longer, then add the tomatoes in their juice. Break up the tomatoes with a spoon, stir, then cover the mixture and simmer gently until the potatoes are tender, about 5–10 minutes.

Add the coconut cream and cauliflower and simmer uncovered for another 5 minutes, or until the cauliflower is tender. Stir in the peas (if using), salt and coriander, and cook for 1–2 minutes longer before adding the quartered or roughly chopped hard-boiled eggs.

This curry is substantial enough to serve alone as a meal for three, but can easily feed four or five adults if served on steamed rice.

NOTE: Omit the eggs for a vegan version.

SPINACH AND MUSHROOM FRITTATA

Frittata is faster to make than a baked square or quiche and can be prepared from ingredients that can be found in almost any kitchen. What could be more convenient than grabbing some eggs and assorted bits and pieces from the fridge and having a meal ready in minutes?

FOR 2–3 SERVINGS:

1 medium-sized onion
3 tablespoons olive or canola oil
1 teaspoon (1–2 cloves) minced garlic, optional
about 250g mushrooms, thickly sliced
4 large eggs
½ cup cottage cheese
250g frozen spinach, thawed and squeezed
2 tablespoons grated parmesan cheese
1–2 tablespoons basil or sun-dried tomato pesto
½ teaspoon salt
pepper to taste

Peel and slice the onion, then heat 1 tablespoon of the oil in a large non-stick frying pan. Add the onion and garlic (if using) and sauté until the onion begins to soften and brown slightly, then add the mushrooms. Continue to cook until these have wilted. Remove from the pan and set aside, then wipe the pan out with a paper towel.

Combine the eggs, cottage cheese, spinach, parmesan cheese, pesto and seasonings together in a small bowl. Add the onion-mushroom mixture and stir gently to combine. Heat the remaining oil in the pan then add the egg mixture. Cook over moderate heat for about 5 minutes, or until the bottom is golden brown. Sprinkle with a little extra parmesan cheese (if desired) and place the pan under a hot grill (leave the handle protruding so it doesn't melt) until the top looks dry and the centre is firm when pressed.

Serve hot or warm, cutting wedges from the pan, or turning out on to a large flat board or plate.

A frittata is a type of substantial omelet. Learn how to make an extra-quick, **French omelet** too, since this can be eaten plain or folded round leftovers, at any time of the day.

Beat 2 eggs with 2 tablespoons of water and a pinch of salt, using a fork. Next, heat a small, non-stick pan with 2 teaspoons of butter. Swirl it round the pan and, when it is straw-coloured, pour in the egg mixture. As it sets, lift its edge, tilt the pan, and let any liquid mixture run underneath. Add warm filling if you like, flip the omelet in half, and serve – it should take a minute in all!

Spinach and Mushroom Frittata

CRISPY (COIN PURSE) EGGS

Alison loves to come back from other countries with new recipes for everyday foods. In San Francisco she learned that there were more ways to fry an egg than 'easy over' and 'sunny side up'! These eggs are purse-shaped, with a soft 'gold coin' inside, and a crispy brown coating, well worth a little practice to perfect.

FOR 1 SERVING:

2 teaspoons canola or olive oil
1 large, fresh egg
pepper and salt or spicy salt (see below)
about a cup of hot cooked rice
sweet chilli sauce (or oyster sauce)
spring onion curls or chopped spring onions

Preheat a wok or a small rounded frying pan over a fairly high heat. Add the oil, and tilt the wok (or pan) to coat a saucer-sized area. When the oil is hot and almost smoking, carefully slide in the egg (previously broken into a small bowl or saucer). Take care doing this, because the egg and hot oil splutter and sizzle. Sprinkle the egg with a little pepper and salt, or with spicy salt (below) as it cooks.

When the bottom and the edges of the egg white are browned and crusty, slide a spatula under half of the egg and flip it over to make a half moon shape. Gently press the edges together until the two sides set and hold the egg in a purse shape.

Lower the heat and cook for 10–20 seconds longer, until the white round the yolk has just set, the yolk is still runny, and the outside surfaces are crispy and brown.

Place a cupful of hot rice on a plate and top with the hot egg. Drizzle with sweet chilli sauce (or oyster sauce if you are a semi-vegetarian). Garnish with spring onion curls, or with chopped spring onions.

NOTES: To make spring onion curls, shred spring onions lengthways. Soak pieces in iced water until they curl.

To make seasoned salt, heat 2 tablespoons Szechwan pepper-corns (from stores selling Oriental foods) on foil under a grill until they smoke slightly. Using a coffee grinder or a mortar and pestle, grind them with 2 tablespoons of salt and a teaspoon of black peppercorns. Keep in an airtight jar.

BEAN-SPROUT EGGS (EGG FOO YOUNG)

Crunchy, lightly cooked, tender bean sprouts, smooth egg and flavourful sauce make a remarkably satisfying combination. Make yourself familiar with this quick and easy recipe so you can make it with speed and confidence. There are many exciting sprouts to choose from – experiment and see which is your favourite.

FOR 4 SERVINGS:

SAUCE
1 tablespoon cornflour
2 teaspoons soy sauce
1 teaspoon vegetable stock powder
1 teaspoon sugar
1 cup water

OMELET
2 cups mung or soy bean sprouts
1–2 cups sliced mushrooms
3–4 spring onions, chopped
cooking oil
3 or 4 eggs
2 tablespoons water
½ teaspoon salt

Make the sauce by mixing the ingredients, in the order given, in a pot. Simmer for 2–3 minutes, then remove from heat and put aside.

For the omelet, sauté first the bean sprouts, then the mushrooms and spring onions, in about 1 tablespoon of oil in a hot pan. Cook just enough to wilt the vegetables. Remove to a flattish dish, mix, then divide into four piles.

Beat together the eggs, water and salt to combine. Pour into a measuring cup. Heat a medium-sized frying pan, add 1 teaspoon oil, then a quarter of the egg mixture. Before this sets sprinkle one quarter of the vegetables over it. Lift edges and let uncooked egg from surface run under the edges to cook. Roll loosely, or fold in quarters, as soon as egg in centre is no longer liquid.

Serve with some of the sauce. Repeat method for other three servings.

Crispy (Coin Purse) Eggs

MEXICAN BEANS AND RICE

It may not be authentic, but this simple and delicious one-pot bean and rice mixture really tastes great!

FOR 4 SERVINGS:

1 medium-sized onion
2 tablespoons olive or canola oil
1 teaspoon (1–2 cloves) minced garlic
1 large green pepper
1 cup long-grain rice
1 teaspoon each ground cumin and oreganum
1/2 teaspoon minced red chilli or chilli powder
300g can tomato purée
1 1/2–2 cups hot water
425g can red kidney beans, drained
2 tablespoons chopped fresh or bottled coriander
1/2–1 teaspoon salt
sour cream (or soy yoghurt) and chopped fresh coriander
  to serve

Dice the onion while the oil heats in a large lidded pan. Add the onion and garlic and sauté until the onion is soft. Dice the pepper then stir it in to the pan and cook, stirring frequently, for 1–2 minutes longer.

Add the rice and stir until it is evenly coated with oil. Cook, stirring frequently, until the rice has turned milky white, then add the cumin, oreganum, chilli, and tomato purée. Pour in 1 1/2 cups of hot water and stir until everything is well combined. Bring the mixture to the boil, then reduce the heat to a gentle simmer and cover. Cook for about 15 minutes or until the rice is just tender, stirring occasionally to make sure the rice doesn't catch on the bottom. If the mixture looks too dry during this time, add another 1/4 cup of water (repeat if necessary).

When the rice is cooked, stir in the beans, coriander and salt to taste. Serve as is, topping each serving with a dollop of sour cream (or soy yoghurt) and a little extra chopped fresh coriander, or use as a filling for enchiladas or burritos.

Keep canned red kidney beans in your store cupboard, so that you can put together easy bean mixtures at short notice. Try leftover bean mixtures added to scrambled eggs and spooned onto tortillas and served as burritos. For **easy scrambled eggs**, beat 2 eggs with 1/4 cup of milk and a pinch of salt in a small clear glass bowl. Microwave on full power for 2–3 minutes, stirring set egg in to the middle every 30 seconds. Stop cooking as soon as the egg mixture sets and increases in volume.

CHEESE BURRITOS

Mexican food is great! For almost instant food, these burritos really do make quite a substantial meal. Simon sometimes omits the beans from the salsa and uses some warmed refried beans instead. Some people will find one burrito ample, while others (like Simon) will manage two!

FOR 3–4 SERVINGS:

SALSA

1 ripe avocado
3 firm ripe tomatoes
425g can red kidney beans
1–2 chopped spring onions
1–2 tablespoons chopped coriander leaf
1 teaspoon ground cumin
1 tablespoon lime or lemon juice
1 tablespoon olive oil
salt and pepper to taste

about 6 flour tortillas
1–1 1/2 cups grated cheese
about 2 cups finely chopped lettuce
sour cream
hot chilli sauce

Turn the grill on to preheat, then prepare the salsa. Peel and cube the avocado, then dice the tomatoes. Stir the prepared avocado and tomatoes through the drained kidney beans, spring onions, coriander, cumin, juice and the oil. Season to taste with salt and pepper.

Working with one or two at a time, sprinkle each tortilla generously with grated cheese. Place them briefly under the grill until the cheese is melted.

To assemble place a generous handful of lettuce in a line down the middle of each tortilla, then add a generous spoonful (or two) of the salsa and top this with a little sour cream and chilli sauce to taste. Fold or roll the edges of the tortilla towards the middle to make a tube and serve immediately.

There is no classy way to eat these, they are best served to family or good friends!

Cheese Burritos

CORN CHIP CASSEROLE

Simon's wife, Sam, makes this delicious but unusual sounding recipe. Cooked like this the corn chips soften and take on a quite different character from Nachos.

FOR 4 SERVINGS:

1 medium-sized onion
2 tablespoons olive or canola oil
1 teaspoon (1–2 cloves) minced garlic
1 red or green pepper
1 teaspoon each ground cumin and oreganum
½ teaspoon minced red chilli or chilli powder
½ teaspoon salt
425g can red kidney beans, drained
1 large avocado, peeled and diced
2–3 tablespoons chopped fresh coriander
juice ½ lemon

SAUCE:

3 tablespoons (25g) butter
3 tablespoons flour
1½ cups milk
1 cup grated tasty cheese
½ teaspoon each ground cumin and oreganum, optional
about 150g corn chips
½ cup grated cheese
paprika to dust

Peel and slice the onion while the oil heats in a large pan. Add the onion and garlic and sauté for 1–2 minutes then chop and add the red or green pepper. Continue to cook, stirring frequently, until the onion is soft and turning clear. Remove the pan from the heat and stir in the seasonings, kidney beans, avocado, coriander and lemon juice. Leave to stand while you prepare the sauce.

Melt the butter in a medium-sized pot, add the flour and stir to make a smooth paste. Cook for 1 minute, stirring continuously, then add half of the milk. Continue stirring until the mixture thickens and comes to the boil, ensuring there are no lumps. Add the remaining milk and let the sauce thicken and boil again. Remove from the heat and stir in the cheese and extra seasonings (if using).

Arrange half of the corn chips in a layer over the bottom of a shallow (25 x 30cm) casserole dish. Cover these with the avocado-bean mixture, then cover this with the remaining corn chips. Pour the cheese sauce evenly over the layered mixture then sprinkle with the additional grated cheese and dust with paprika. Bake at 220°C for 10–15 minutes or until the top is golden brown.

Serve alone or with rice and a shredded lettuce or tomato salad.

Corn Chip Casserole

CHICKPEA AND PUMPKIN CASSEROLE

This is a really delicious casserole. It has been popular with our family for years, but was somehow omitted from both Meals Without Meat *and* Meals Without Red Meat – *it's time to put this right! We used to make it from dried chickpeas, but it is really easy if you use canned ones instead.*

FOR 6 LARGE SERVINGS:

750 g peeled and deseeded pumpkin
1 large onion
1 teaspoon (1–2 cloves) minced garlic
50g butter
6–8 drops Tabasco sauce
2 cups grated tasty cheese
½–1 teaspoon salt
black pepper
2 x 310g cans chickpeas, drained and rinsed

Turn the oven on to preheat to 180°C.

Cut the pumpkin into cubes and simmer in a little water until tender.

Chop the onion, sauté with the garlic in butter until transparent, then mash with the drained pumpkin, keeping mixture slightly chunky.

Mix in the Tabasco sauce and cheese. Taste after adding the cheese and add salt and pepper to taste. Gently stir in the drained chickpeas.

Spread the mixture in a large (23 x 23cm) non-stick sprayed or lightly oiled baking pan and heat through at 180°C until bubbly at edges and hot in the centre.

COOKING DRIED BEANS:

To save time all our recipes have used canned beans, but of course, if you have time, you can soak and cook dried beans and use these instead (a 425g can holds 1¾ cups of cooked beans). There are two basic soaking methods, overnight or rapid. Simply cover beans with plenty of warm water (1 cup beans to 1 litre water) and leave to stand for at least 4 hours (or overnight), or for a rapid soak, cover the beans with plenty of hot water, bring them to the boil, then remove them from the heat and leave to stand for 2 hours. Drain soaked beans, cover with clean water and boil until tender, 20–60 minutes depending on the type of bean used.

NOTE: Red kidney beans must be boiled rapidly for at least 10 minutes.

BUTTER CHICKPEAS

Simon loves Indian food, and this is his vegetarian version of 'Butter Chicken'. The sauce is so good it could be served with almost anything and be a hit, but chickpeas and new potatoes work really well. (Paneer cheese is also delicious.)

FOR 2–3 LARGE SERVINGS:

1 medium-sized onion
2 tablespoons canola oil
1 teaspoon (1–2 cloves) minced garlic
2 teaspoons each curry powder and garam masala
1 teaspoon each ground ginger and cumin
300g can condensed tomato soup
1/2 cup cream
300g can chickpeas
200g boiled new potatoes, cubed
1–2 tablespoons chopped coriander leaf, fresh or bottled
1/2 teaspoon salt

Chop the onion very finely while the oil heats in a large pan. Add the onion and garlic and cook, stirring frequently, until the onion is beginning to brown. Stir in the curry powder and garam masala, ginger, and cumin. Continue to cook, stirring frequently, for one to two minutes longer.

Tip in the soup, cream, drained chickpeas and potatoes and leave the sauce to simmer for about 5 minutes. Add the chopped coriander and salt to taste.

Serve over steamed basmati rice accompanied with naan bread (this can now be found in the frozen foods section of some supermarkets) and a selection of chutneys and/or pickles.

Chickpeas or garbanzo beans seem to have found their way into the traditional cuisine of many different races and cultures around the world. This is no mean feat and is probably not only because of their delicious, nutty flavour, but also because they are so versatile and nutritious. The humble chickpea is low in fat, rich in fibre, complex carbohydrate, and protein and is a good source of calcium, iron and B vitamins.

CHICKPEA AND SPINACH CURRY

This dish has it all – not only is it easy and delicious, it is a complete meal (although Simon likes it served with rice and naan), and it's relatively low in fat and high in fibre. Simon loves the flavour of cumin so he adds the extra, but it can be left out with no drastic effect.

FOR 4 LARGE SERVINGS:

250g packet frozen spinach, thawed
2 tablespoons canola oil
1–2 teaspoons each minced ginger and garlic
1 medium-large onion, finely chopped
2–3 teaspoons curry powder (mild or hot)
2 teaspoons garam masala
1/2–1 teaspoon cumin seeds, optional
2–3 bay leaves
400g can whole tomatoes in juice
2–3 medium-sized (250g) potatoes, cut into 1cm cubes
310g can chickpeas, drained
1/4–1/2 cup water, if required
1/2–1 teaspoon salt
black pepper
2 tablespoons chopped coriander leaf, fresh or bottled

Thaw the spinach (microwave for 6–8 minutes at 30% power), but do not drain.

Heat the oil in a large pan, add the ginger and garlic, using amounts you like, and the onion. Stir-fry until the onion has softened and is turning clear. Add the curry powder, garam masala, cumin (if using) and bay leaves. Cook for 1 minute then add the spinach with its liquid and the tomatoes in juice. Crush and break up the tomatoes, then stir in the cubed potatoes and the chickpeas.

Simmer the mixture gently for 15 minutes, or until the potato is tender, adding a little of the water if the mixture begins to look too dry. When the potatoes are cooked, season to taste with salt and pepper and add the chopped coriander leaf.

Chickpea and Spinach Curry

BREAD TOPPED BEAN CASSEROLE

We wrote this recipe with cold winter evenings in mind – there is something very warming about the way the rich dark filling hides under a crisp golden crust. Don't be put off by the fearsome-looking list of ingredients, it really is very simple!

FOR 4 LARGE SERVINGS:

1 large onion
1 medium-large carrot
2 tablespoons olive or canola oil
2 teaspoons (1–2 cloves) minced garlic
1 red or green (or ½ each) pepper
6 brown mushrooms
1 teaspoon sugar
1 tablespoon flour
½ cup water
1 tablespoon tomato paste
½ teaspoon dried basil
¼ teaspoon dried thyme
425g can red kidney beans, drained
½–1 teaspoon salt
black pepper to taste
½ loaf french bread
1–2 tablespoons oil
½–1 cup grated cheese

Turn the oven to 225°C to preheat.

Peel, quarter and slice the onion and slice the carrot while the oil heats in a large pan. Add the onion, garlic and carrot and cook, stirring frequently, until the onion is soft and clear. While the onion mixture cooks, deseed and slice the pepper and quarter the mushrooms. Add the sugar, pepper and mushrooms and continue to cook, stirring frequently, until the onions have browned. Stir in the flour and cook for a minute longer, then add the water, tomato paste and herbs. Mix in the beans and season to taste with salt and pepper. Simmer gently for about 5 minutes then transfer the vegetable mixture to a lightly oiled or non-stick sprayed 20 x 25cm casserole dish. (The filling can be prepared ahead to this stage.)

Cut the french bread into 1cm-thick slices, and pour the oil into a small shallow dish or saucer. Lightly dip one side of each slice of bread into the oil (it should just be moistened with oil, not soaked) and arrange the slices oiled side up over the top of the filling mixture, until it is all covered.

Sprinkle the bread topping with the grated cheese, using more or less to taste, then bake at 225°C for 10–15 minutes until the filling is hot and the crust golden brown. Serve with some lightly cooked winter vegetables (or even a salad), and some bread or mashed potatoes.

VARIATION: Chopping (in a food processor) or mashing the filling mixture may make it more appealing to those who are 'non-bean' oriented.

CURRIED RED LENTIL DAHL

We don't know exactly what makes this version of dahl so good, but it really is – even those who would normally turn their noses up at the thought of red lentils have been seen coming back for more!

FOR 3–4 LARGE SERVINGS:

1 tablespoon olive or canola oil
1 large onion, diced
1 teaspoon (1–2 cloves) minced garlic
1 large bay leaf
1 teaspoon minced red chilli or chilli powder
2 teaspoons each curry powder and turmeric
2 teaspoons each mustard and cumin seeds
1 cup split red lentils
2 cups water or 2 teaspoons vegetable stock powder and
    2 cups of water
½–1 teaspoon salt to taste
1–2 tablespoons chopped coriander leaf, fresh or bottled

Heat the oil in a large pan, add the onion and garlic and cook, stirring frequently, until the onion has softened and is turning clear. Add the bay leaf and spices and cook, stirring continuously, for 1–2 minutes longer.

Tip in the lentils and the water or stock, bring the mixture to the boil, then reduce the heat to a gentle simmer and cook until the lentils are tender, about 20–25 minutes.

Stir in the coriander and serve accompanied by your selection/s of steamed rice, naan bread, poppadoms and/or Spiced Tomato and Cucumber Salad (see page 45).

Bread Topped Bean Casserole

RED BEAN BURGERS

As long as you have a food processor, you can make these burgers very quickly. Shaping and coating them can be a bit awkward because the uncooked mixture is soft but, by the time your burgers are in buns, covered with ketchup, who's going to notice they aren't perfect!

FOR 3–4 SERVINGS:

½ small onion
1 slice firm-textured bread
½ teaspoon (1 clove) minced garlic
1 large egg
¼ cup finely grated parmesan cheese
425g can red kidney beans
1 teaspoon ground cumin, optional
1 tablespoon sun-dried tomato pesto, optional
1 teaspoon balsamic vinegar, optional

COATING:
3 slices (crusts will do) stale bread
1 large egg

Before you wet the food processor, crumb the bread for the coating and put aside in a shallow dish. Chop the quartered onion, bread (broken in several pieces) and the garlic in the food processor. Add to this mixture the egg and the parmesan cheese.

Tip the beans from the can into a sieve. Drain and rinse them well, since any bean liquid will make the burgers softer. Add to the food processor with any or all of the optional ingredients. Process in bursts until the beans are fairly finely chopped (but not a smooth purée) and the mixture is just firm enough to shape into four to six even-sized balls with wet hands.

Using a fork, beat the egg for the coating in a shallow bowl until the white and yolk are well combined. Heat a pan with enough oil to cover the bottom. Turn each ball first in the crumbs, then in the egg, then in the crumbs again. Flatten to make patties about 10cm across, place each in the pan as it is ready and cook thicker burgers over fairly low heat for 5 minutes per side, and thinner burgers for 3–4 minutes per side. Eat straight away or reheat on a barbecue.

Serve in buns with your favourite hamburger trimmings, or serve with gravy and cooked vegetables.

VARIATION: If you don't have a food processor, replace the bread in the burgers with 3 tablespoons fine dry breadcrumbs, grate the onion, and mash the beans then mix everything with a fork. Use egg and fine dry breadcrumbs for the coating.

NOTE: These 'burgers' are solid enough to be cooked ahead to be reheated as a vegetarian option at a barbecue.

CHEESE & ONION 'SAUSAGES'

These sausages are quick and surprisingly like the meat version. Once cooked they are quite firm, but they are fairly soft until this time. If you want to barbecue them, use a well-oiled hot plate or grill and handle very gently.

FOR 3 SERVINGS (6 SAUSAGES):

1 small-medium onion
1½ cups grated cheese
3 cups (150g) soft breadcrumbs (crumbled bread)
½ teaspoon salt
¼ teaspoon each sage and thyme
black pepper to taste
2 large eggs
about ¼ cup dry breadcrumbs to coat

Chop the onion very finely (a food processor does this well). Mix onion together with the grated cheese, breadcrumbs and seasonings. Add one of the eggs, then separate the other, adding the yolk to the crumb mixture and reserving the white. Stir until well combined.

Using wet hands, shape the mixture into six even-sized sausages (if the mixture is too wet and sticky, add 1–2 tablespoons of the dry breadcrumbs and mix again). As each sausage is completed, roll it first in the egg white, then in the dry breadcrumbs. Leave to stand for at least 5 minutes, then cook in a well-oiled pan until golden brown on all sides (6–8 minutes).

Serve with salad or vegetables, or as you would conventional sausages.

VEGETARIAN GRAVY:
In a medium-sized non-stick frying pan heat 2 tablespoons butter with 2 tablespoons flour over moderate heat, stirring often, for 2–3 minutes or until the mixture is lightly browned.

Stir in 1 cup vegetable stock (or 1 teaspoon stock powder and 1 cup water) or the lightly salted water in which vegetables have been boiled. Stir until the mixture thickens and is smooth. Add a few drops of soy sauce if the mixture is not brown enough. Thin with more water or stock if too thick. Taste and adjust seasoning, adding a pinch of sugar if necessary.

Cheese and Onion 'Sausages'

EASY RATATOUILLE

Every autumn, we get the urge to make a big, strongly flavoured vegetable stew which we enjoy for several meals, each seeming better than the last. This short-cut version, which takes 45 minutes, is excellent.

FOR 6–8 SERVINGS:

¼ cup olive oil
2 medium-sized eggplants
4 red, orange or yellow peppers
4 green and/or yellow zucchini
4 large onions
1½ teaspoons (2 cloves) minced garlic
up to ¼ cup extra olive oil
2 (400g) cans whole tomatoes in juice
2 teaspoons sugar
1 teaspoon salt
2 tablespoons basil pesto
2–3 tablespoons chopped fresh herbs

Make this in the largest, heaviest (lidded) pot, frying pan or flame-proof casserole dish that you have. Heat the first measure of olive oil in it and add the unpeeled eggplant, sliced peppers, and zucchini, all cut in 2cm chunky pieces. Cook over medium to high heat for 15 minutes, so that the vegetables brown lightly but do not steam in large amounts of watery juices. Add the onions chopped into similar-sized pieces, the garlic, and enough extra oil to stop the mixture sticking or burning. Raise the heat slightly, and cook for 15 minutes longer, until the onions are transparent and lightly browned, too.

Stir in the tomatoes (and juice), add the sugar, salt and pesto, and bring to the boil with the lid ajar. Cook on medium heat so the liquid bubbles and thickens, but the vegetables do not burn. We like the stew at the stage where the liquid is quite thick but the vegetables still have some firmness, after about 15 minutes simmering. Taste and adjust seasoning.

Serve in bowls, with chunks of firm, crusty bread, as a complete meal, or serve on pasta or rice, topped with parmesan cheese, or ladle generous amounts into a pot of cooked, drained, firm potatoes, heat through, and serve in bowls.

VARIATION: To reduce cooking time, use less oil, and for maximum flavour, brush the thickly sliced eggplant with olive oil and brown in a double-sided contact grill (see page 8). Repeat with the halved peppers and zucchini and thickly sliced onions. When browned, cut in cubes and simmer with the remaining ingredients, as above.

EASY TWICE-BAKED POTATOES

If you have to use a conventional oven, twice-baked potatoes do take quite a while, however, microwaving them for the first 'baking' really speeds things up. If you do have a microwave, you can even put the potatoes on to cook while you head off to work in the morning!

FOR 2–4 SERVINGS:

4 large potatoes (about 1kg total)
1 cup cottage cheese
125g creamy blue cheese
2–3 tablespoons chopped fresh dill
½ teaspoon salt
black pepper to taste

Scrub the potatoes then microwave bake them (12–15 minutes on high), turning them once during cooking. To cook in a regular oven, bake for about 1 hour at 180°C. The potatoes are cooked when they are soft when squeezed.

Leave the cooked potatoes to cool, or, working carefully holding the hot potatoes with an oven-mitt or clean teatowel, cut off and discard a thin slice from the long side of each potato. Scoop the insides of the potatoes out leaving a 'shell' about 1cm thick, transferring the flesh to a medium-sized bowl.

Mash the insides together with the cottage cheese, blue cheese, dill and salt and pepper to taste.

Refill the shells with the stuffing mixture, heaping it up into each as required. Bake at 200°C for about 15 minutes, or until the filling mixture is bubbly and beginning to brown.

A simple **baked potato** can form the basis of a delicious meal! Look for extra-large (baking) potatoes when you are shopping. These can be microwaved or conventionally baked (as described in the first part of the recipe above) then filled and served with any of the following, alone or in combinations: pesto mixed with sour cream or cream cheese, leftover salsa or guacamole, chutney or relish, grated cheese, creamed corn, or (of course) baked beans. Top with a handful of crisp sprouts to make it something really special.

Easy Ratatouille

KUMARA AND CORN CAKES

Alison usually gives these an Asian, lightly curried flavour and serves them with Sesame Coleslaw. At times, however, she replaces the curry and coriander with basil or sun-dried tomato pesto and makes equally delicious cakes with quite a different flavour.

FOR 3–4 SERVINGS:

500 g (2 large) kumara
3–4 spring onions, chopped
about 1 cup whole kernel corn, drained
1–2 teaspoons green curry paste
about 1 teaspoon salt
2–3 tablespoons chopped fresh or bottled coriander
2 large eggs
about 1/4 cup self-raising flour

Cut the ends off the kumara, and microwave on full power, turning once, for 6 minutes or until flesh feels soft all over when pressed. When cool enough to handle, peel off the outer skin then mash with a fork. (You should have about 3 cupfuls.)

Add the chopped spring onions, drained corn, curry paste, salt and coriander leaves. (The larger amount of curry paste makes patties hotter than most children would enjoy.) Stir in the unbeaten eggs using a fork, then add enough flour to hold the mixture together, until you can spoon the mixture into 12 rough-surfaced patties using a dessert spoon.

Drop four or six of these into a non-stick pan with the bottom barely covered with hot oil. Cook uncovered over moderate heat for 3–5 minutes, until nicely browned, then turn and cook the other side. Keep warm while cooking the remaining patties, then serve immediately.

VARIATIONS: You can use more or less kumara, corn and spring onions, adding more or less flour to hold the cakes together.

Leave out the curry paste and coriander and add 2 tablespoons basil pesto or sun-dried tomato pesto for cakes with quite a different flavour.

Don't forget that a salad and a chunk of good bread (or a roll) can turn a simple main into an interesting and well-balanced meal. For a really **simple salad** buy a tub of mesclun (mixed baby salad greens) when you are shopping, keep this in the fridge, removing handfuls of the tender leaves as required. To prepare, toss as much mesclun as you need with a squeeze of lemon juice, a dash of olive oil and a grind of salt and pepper, then serve.

FIVE MINUTE MUSHROOMS

This recipe, a favourite of Alison's, must be made with brown, flat or cup-shaped mushrooms (or mature meadow mushrooms), which are 'meaty' and satisfying, with an excellent flavour. Cook them on high heat, making minor changes if you like, for a great 5 minute meal.

FOR 2 LARGE SERVINGS:

400g flat brown or cup-shaped mushrooms
2–3 teaspoons olive oil
2–3 teaspoons butter
1 teaspoon minced garlic
1/2 cup stock or 1/2 teaspoon vegetable stock powder
    in 1/2 cup water
1/4 teaspoon minced red chilli or chilli powder
1/4 teaspoon thyme, crumbled
freshly ground black pepper
1 teaspoon flour
1 tomato, optional
pinch salt
1–2 tablespoons fresh or sour cream, optional

Trim the mushrooms so edges of caps are level with the stalks. (This makes it easier to brown the undersides.)

Heat the oil and butter in a heavy frying pan. Add the garlic and mushrooms, rounded sides down, and brown over high heat. Turn mushrooms over, add about half the stock, cover, then shake the pan so the mushrooms wilt in the steam and brown on their undersides too. Keep the heat high enough to evaporate the stock.

Remove the lid, lower the heat a little, then add the chilli, thyme, and a good grinding of black pepper. Sprinkle the flour over the mushrooms, turn them over, then add the finely cubed tomato and remaining stock.

Add more liquid if necessary, to finish up with mushrooms glazed in lightly thickened liquid. Add a little fresh or sour cream if you like. Heat again, adjust seasonings, and sprinkle with chopped herbs.

Serve on toast, on a toasted split roll, on pasta, or as you would serve a stew.

HINT:
It is not a good idea to refrigerate mushrooms in plastic bags. Paper bags or calico bags allow the mushrooms to breathe and stop them getting a slimy coating in the refrigerator.

Five Minute Mushrooms

EGGPLANT STACKS

This is an interesting and delicious way to use eggplant. This recipe gives quantities to serve two adults, but it is very easy to just multiply for larger numbers.

FOR 2 SERVINGS:

1 medium-sized eggplant
2–3 tablespoons olive oil
salt and pepper
2–3 tablespoons chopped fresh basil (or 2 tablespoons basil pesto)
2–3 medium-sized tomatoes, thinly sliced
6–8 black olives, chopped, optional
100g thinly sliced (or 1 cup grated) mozzarella cheese

Turn the oven on to preheat to 200°C. Cut the eggplant lengthways into six even slices. Lay these on a baking tray, and drizzle lightly with olive oil, then turn them over and do the same to the other side. Sprinkle lightly with salt and pepper, then bake for 12–15 minutes, until soft and beginning to brown.

Sprinkle each of the slices with some of the chopped basil, or brush with pesto, then cover the four larger slices with sliced tomato. Sprinkle the chopped olives, if using, over the tomato then put the sliced or grated cheese over these. Sprinkle lightly with salt and pepper.

Re-assemble the eggplant in halves by stacking the slices (smallest pieces on top!), more or less as they were cut. Sprinkle each half with any remaining cheese then bake at 200°C for another 10–15 minutes until the cheese has melted and the tomato looks cooked.

Serve with a green salad and crusty bread.

VARIATION: Alison loves these baked for twice the time after the layers are assembled. They don't look as good but they taste marvellous!

A double-sided contact grill will **brown eggplant slices** in 5–10 minutes, using considerably less oil than any other method we have tried. If you have a contact grill, brown the eggplant used in Eggplant Stacks in several batches while the oven heats. As with other new appliances, you should experiment, cooking a variety of different foods in it, to find as many uses as possible for it.

KUMARA AND POTATO CAKES WITH MANGO SALSA

The crisp little kumara and potato cakes really come to life when served with our delicious mango salsa!

FOR 2–3 SERVINGS:

150–200g kumara
150–200g potatoes
2 spring onions
1 large egg
1/2 teaspoon salt
black pepper
about 1/4 cup oil for cooking

SALSA:

400g can mango slices in light syrup or 1 cup finely chopped fresh mango
1 spring onion
1 tablespoon lemon (or lime) juice
1/2 teaspoon minced red chilli or chilli powder
1/2 teaspoon salt
1–2 tablespoons chopped coriander leaf

Scrub the kumara and potatoes, then grate with the skins on (if you use the smaller quantity of one, use the larger quantity of the other so total remains 350g). Place the grated mixture in a bowl and cover with water. Leave to stand for 1–2 minutes, then twist and squeeze dry in a clean teatowel, squeezing out as much water as you can. Put back in the dried bowl.

Thinly slice the spring onions add these to the grated mixture along with the egg, salt and a generous grind of black pepper, then stir lightly with a fork to combine (do not overmix). Leave the mixture to stand while you prepare the salsa.

Drain the mango slices and cut the flesh into 5mm cubes. Thinly slice the spring onion then mix with the cubed mango, lemon or lime juice, chilli, salt and chopped coriander in a small bowl.

Heat the oil in a large non-stick pan. Gently drop generous dessertspoonfuls of the kumara-potato mixture into the pan, flattening them into cakes about 1 cm thick. Cook over medium-high heat for 3–4 minutes per side, or until crisp and golden brown.

Drain the cooked cakes briefly on several layers of paper towels, then arrange on plates and serve topped with a generous dollop of the salsa, and a green salad.

Eggplant Stacks

STUFFED MUSHROOMS

These tasty stuffed mushrooms are very versatile – use more, smaller mushrooms to serve them as a starter or finger food, or fewer large flat mushrooms to serve as a main course. Either way, the filling can be prepared ahead in minutes and the mushrooms baked when required.

FOR 3–4 LARGE SERVINGS OR 6–8 STARTERS:

2 slices wholemeal bread
1 clove garlic, peeled
1 tablespoon olive oil
1 tablespoon basil pesto
1 tablespoon grated parmesan cheese
2–3 tablespoons chopped black olives
¼ teaspoon thyme
¼–½ teaspoon salt
¼ cup pine nuts
8 large (10–12cm) flat brown, or 12–16 smaller (6–8cm)
   mushrooms
black pepper to taste

Turn the oven on to preheat to 225°C.

Tear the bread into smaller pieces and crumb in a food processor. Add the garlic and process briefly. Add the next six ingredients and process until just mixed (the mixture should stay as crumbs, not turn to paste). Tip in the pine nuts and whiz again to mix evenly.

Remove and discard the mushroom stems. Arrange the mushrooms (gills up) in a single layer over the bottom of a sponge roll tin or roasting pan. Spoon the filling into the caps, dividing it evenly between the mushrooms and leaving it sitting 'fluffed-up' rather than packed down.

Bake at 220°C for 12–15 minutes, or until the filling is golden brown. Remove from the oven and leave to stand for about 5 minutes before serving alone or with Vegetarian Gravy (see page 88).

Raclette is a Swiss tradition, and makes an easy and delicious meal. In the traditional approach, boiled potatoes and pickled cucumbers are served smothered in melted raclette cheese, scraped off a large wheel of cheese heated in front of a fire or under a special grill. Delicious raclette cheese is now produced in New Zealand, and slices of this can be melted on a flat plate (under a conventional grill, or in the microwave), then slid off on to potatoes, pickles, bread or other foods of your choosing.

THAI CURRIED VEGETABLE-NOODLE STEW

This tasty vegetable curry is somewhere between a soup and a 'traditional' curry. Despite a long list of ingredients, it is simple as the vegetables and noodles are simmered and served together in a spicy peanut and coconut cream sauce.

FOR 2–3 LARGE SERVINGS:

100g rice sticks or noodles
1 medium-sized onion
1 tablespoon canola oil
1 teaspoon each minced garlic and ginger
2 tablespoons red curry paste
2–3 small potatoes
400g can coconut cream
1 cup vegetable stock
3–4 tablespoons peanut butter
1 teaspoon each salt and sugar
1 small eggplant
½ each red and green pepper (or one of either)
2 medium-sized zucchini
100g brown button mushrooms
1–2 tablespoons Kikkoman soy sauce
2–3 tablespoons chopped fresh or bottled coriander
100g soy or mung bean sprouts

Cut or break the noodles into 10cm lengths, put them in a large bowl and cover them with boiling water. Leave to stand while you prepare the curry.

Peel, halve and slice the onion. Heat the oil in a large pot or wok, add the onion, the minced garlic and ginger and the red curry paste and stir-fry for 1–2 minutes. Cut the potatoes into 1cm cubes and add these with the coconut cream, stock, peanut butter, salt and sugar.

Bring the mixture to the boil, then reduce the heat to a gentle simmer and cook for 10 minutes, stirring occasionally. While the potatoes simmer, cube the eggplant, deseed and slice the peppers, cut the zucchini into 1cm slices and halve the mushrooms. Add these vegetables and the drained rice noodles to the pot, then simmer until the potatoes and vegetables are just tender (about 10 minutes).

Add soy sauce to taste, then the coriander and the bean sprouts (reserve a few to use as a garnish). Serve ladled into large bowls and topped with a few bean sprouts. Bowls of chopped roasted peanuts, minced chillies and chopped coriander leaf also make good accompaniments.

NOTES: Unless cooking for semi-vegetarians, check that your curry paste does not contain shrimp paste.

Thai Curried Vegetable-Noodle Stew

AVOCADO FLAN

This unusual flan makes a good talking point and has a delicate and interesting flavour. Try it next time you want something a little different and see nice avocados on sale.

FOR 3–4 SERVINGS:

1 large avocado
1 cup cottage cheese
2 large eggs
½ teaspoon salt
3 spring onions
1 cup mashed potato
¼ cup grated parmesan cheese
4 sheets filo pastry
1 tablespoon olive or other oil
1 or 2 avocados for decoration, optional

Preheat the oven to 200°C.

Halve the avocado and scoop the flesh into a large mixing bowl. Mash with a fork. Add the cottage cheese, eggs and salt and mix into the avocado. Chop the leaves as well as the stems of the spring onions. Add these, the mashed potato and the parmesan cheese and stir well to mix everything.

Open the packet of filo pastry, remove four sheets (and seal and refrigerate the remainder). Brush three sheets of filo lightly with oil and stack them. Put the unoiled sheet on top. Ease the stacked sheets into a 23cm flan tin or pie plate, then fold the edges in and under to form the edge of the pie.

Turn the avocado mixture into the unbaked pastry shell, level the top, and bake at 200°C for 10 minutes, until pastry is golden brown, then turn down to 180°C and bake for about 20 minutes longer, until the centre feels firm.

Serve warm, plain or topped with overlapping thin slices of avocado. (Dip these in lemon juice first, to stop them browning.) Salsa Fresca (see page 31) or Mango Salsa (see page 95) spooned over each slice of pie is delicious.

VARIATION: Replace the filo pastry with a sheet of pre-rolled pastry, trimming the edge to fit the baking dish.

HINT:
For quick mashed potato, cut a large scrubbed potato into 1cm cubes and microwave in an oven bag with 1 tablespoon water for 3–4 minutes, or until tender. Drain off any remaining water and squeeze bag to mash potatoes.

EGGPLANT AND MUSHROOM CASSEROLE

This dish does require several different steps during its preparation, however, individually they are all so simple (and the results so delicious) we think it warrants inclusion in this book.

FOR 4 LARGE SERVINGS:

2 medium-sized or 1 large eggplant
2–3 tablespoons olive or canola oil
1 medium-sized onion
1 tablespoon olive oil
1 teaspoon (1–2 cloves) minced garlic
250g mushrooms, sliced
1–2 tablespoons basil pesto
½–1 teaspoon salt
black pepper to taste
1 cup sour cream or plain unsweetened yoghurt
1 large egg
½ teaspoon salt
½–1 cup grated tasty cheese

Preheat the oven to 200°C. Cut the eggplant/s into 1cm thick slices, brush both sides lightly with oil and arrange the slices in a single layer on one or two baking sheets. Place these in the oven and bake for 15–20 minutes, until the eggplant is soft and beginning to brown at the edges. (If you have to use two trays, swap their position in the oven after 10 minutes so the eggplant cooks evenly).

While the eggplant bakes, peel and slice the onion then heat the oil in a large (non-stick) frying pan. Add the garlic and onion and sauté, stirring frequently, until the onion has softened. Stir in the sliced mushrooms and cook gently until the mushrooms have wilted. Add the pesto, salt and pepper to taste and cook for 1–2 minutes longer, then remove from the heat.

Lightly oil or non-stick spray a 25 x 30cm casserole dish. Arrange half the baked eggplant slices in a layer over the bottom of the casserole dish, cover this with the mushroom mixture, then another layer of the eggplant slices.

Mix the sour cream or yoghurt, egg and salt together in a small bowl. Pour and spread this mixture over the layered mixture, then sprinkle the top with the grated cheese.

Bake at 200°C for 20 minutes or until the top is bubbly and turning brown. Remove from the oven and leave to stand for 5–10 minutes. Serve with a salad or lightly cooked vegetables and some crusty bread.

Avocado Flan

MUSHROOM AND POTATO PIE

This 'single crust' pie is simple and makes a great winter meal – its impressive appearance is matched by its delicious flavour!

FOR 4 SERVINGS:

500g (3–4 medium-sized) potatoes
1 medium-sized onion
2 tablespoons olive or canola oil
1 teaspoon (1–2 cloves) minced garlic
200g brown mushroom stuffing caps
½ teaspoon dried basil (or 1 tablespoon basil pesto)
¼ teaspoon thyme
½ teaspoon salt
black pepper to taste
1 cup (250g) sour cream
½ teaspoon salt
black pepper
1–2 sheets pre-rolled flaky pastry
milk or lightly beaten egg to glaze

Turn the oven on to preheat to 220°C.

Scrub the potatoes, then cut them into 5mm slices. Place them in an oven bag or covered microwave dish and cook on full power for 10 minutes, stirring gently after 5 minutes. (Alternatively, boil the potato slices until just tender, handling them gently to avoid breaking them up.)

Peel and slice the onion while the oil heats in a large frying pan. Add the onion and garlic and sauté until the onion is soft and turning clear. While the onion cooks, slice the mushrooms, then add these to the pan along with the herbs, salt and pepper. Cook, stirring frequently, until the mushrooms have wilted.

While the oven heats, non-stick spray or lightly oil a 20 x 25cm (or round) casserole or deep pie dish. Arrange half of the potato slices evenly over the bottom of the dish, then cover this with the mushroom mixture and then the remaining potato slices. Stir together the sour cream and the remaining salt and pepper. Pour this mixture evenly over the potato-mushroom mixture.

Roll out the pastry (if necessary), until it will cover the casserole/pie dish. Lay the pastry gently over the filling mixture, trimming off any excess. Decorate the edge by patterning it with the tines of a fork and puncture the pastry at 5cm intervals over the surface. Brush with a little milk or beaten egg to glaze, then bake at 220°C for about 15 minutes until the pastry is golden brown.

Serve with a salad or cooked vegetables and some crusty bread.

MEDITERRANEAN VEGETABLE PIE

This versatile pie is good when made with roasted peppers, eggplant, red onion or zucchini, or a mixture of these. For ease and speed, we 'roast' our vegetables easily and fast on a double-sided contact grill (see page 8).

FOR 5–6 SERVINGS:

2 large red, orange or yellow peppers or vegetables
   mentioned above
2 tablespoons olive oil
1 teaspoon (1–2 cloves) minced garlic
2 tablespoons capers, chopped black olives, or vegetarian
   tapenade, optional
1 cup (250g carton) cottage cheese
250g feta cheese, crumbled
4 eggs, lightly beaten
½ teaspoon grated nutmeg
freshly ground black pepper to taste
8 sheets filo pastry
2–3 tablespoons grated parmesan cheese
olive oil for brushing
sesame or poppy seeds, optional

Cut the peppers into three or four large pieces lengthways. Remove the pith and seeds and turn in the olive oil mixed with the garlic, in a shallow roasting pan. Roast uncovered, at 200°C for about 20 minutes, until skin darkens slightly, or cook in a contact grill on high for 5–10 minutes. Cool and peel off darkened skin. (Roast other vegetables in slices, similarly.)

Combine the capers, olives or tapenade (if using), cottage cheese, crumbled feta, eggs, nutmeg, and black pepper. (Do not add any salt.) Mix well, mashing with a fork. (Do not mix in a food processor as the mixture gets too runny.)

Take four sheets of filo pastry, brush each with a little olive oil and sprinkle with grated parmesan. Stack them and place in a roasting or other baking pan big enough to hold the sheets with their edges turned up about 2cm.

Pour in half the filling, then add half the roasted vegetables, the remaining filling and other vegetables.

Prepare the rest of the filo as before and use to cover the pie. Cut smaller or wrinkle the filo top so it fits to the edge. Fold the edges of the filo from the bottom of the pie, over the top. Brush lightly with oil and sprinkle the top with sesame or poppy seeds if you like.

Bake at 190°C for 30–45 minutes. If the pastry browns too quickly, cover with foil for part of the baking time. Serve warm, with a leafy salad and crusty bread.

Mediterranean Vegetable Pie

COUNTRY ONION PIE

This pie looks attractive and tastes particularly interesting because the onions are roasted before they are put in the crust, then surrounded with a creamy mixture flavoured with nutmeg or caraway seeds.

FOR A 20CM PIE, 2–3 SERVINGS:

200g bought pastry
12–15 small (pickling) onions
olive oil
¼ cup sour cream
1 egg
¼ cup milk
¼ teaspoon salt
¼ teaspoon freshly grated nutmeg or ½ teaspoon
   caraway seeds
freshly ground pepper to taste

Thaw the pastry if necessary.

Preheat the oven to 200°C. Cut the root and stem ends off the onions, place them in a bowl or jug, and pour boiling water over them. After a minute, pour off the water and peel off the outer skins which should be soft and easy to remove in one or two pieces. (Do not peel off more layers than you need, or you will not have enough onion to fill the pie.)

Cut onions in half crossways, pour a dribble of olive oil in a heavy roasting pan, put the onions in this cut side down and roast for 15–20 minutes, or until lightly browned. (If you have one, cook halved onions on a double-sided contact grill (see page 8) at Medium, for about 10 minutes.)

Roll pastry out thinly on a floured board and trim off uneven edges to form a 25cm circle. Ease the pastry into a 20cm pie plate, turn under the pastry edges, then pinch or decorate the outer rim as desired.

Combine the remaining ingredients in a food processor, or mix them in a bowl, using an egg beater. (For a stronger caraway flavour, crush the caraway seeds first.) Arrange the cooked onions, larger cut sides up, in the unbaked pie shell. Gently pour the filling around the onions until only their tops are visible. Sprinkle lightly with extra caraway seeds if you like.

Bake at 200°C for 15–20 minutes or until the pastry is evenly browned and the filling is set. Turn down the heat if the crust browns too much before this time. Serve warm, as suggested above.

VARIATION: Use four sheets of filo pastry for the crust, following instructions for Avocado Flan (see page 99).

SPINACH AND FETA FILO PIE

This is loosely based on Greek Spanakopita, but is even easier. Served hot, warm or cold this makes a great summer dish, but by using frozen spinach, it can be made at any time of year.

FOR 4–6 SERVINGS:

1 medium-sized onion
1 tablespoon olive oil
¼ cup pine nuts
500g frozen spinach, thawed
200g feta cheese, crumbled
¼ teaspoon dried basil
¼ teaspoon thyme
¼–½ teaspoon freshly grated nutmeg
½ teaspoon salt
black pepper to taste
2 eggs
8–10 sheets filo pastry
about 2 tablespoons melted butter or olive oil

Turn the oven on to preheat to 200°C.

Peel and slice the onion while you heat the oil in a medium-sized pan. Add the onion and cook until softened, then stir in the pine nuts and continue to cook until these are golden brown.

While the onion cooks squeeze as much liquid as you can from the thawed spinach. Place the spinach in a large bowl and add the crumbled cheese, then the herbs and seasonings and the onion-pine nut mixture. Add the eggs and stir until well mixed.

Non-stick spray or lightly oil a shallow casserole dish (about 20 x 25cm). Lay two sheets of filo out on the bench, and brush the top sheet lightly with melted butter or olive oil. Lay these sheets lengthways down the prepared dish, gently pressing them into the bottom; leave the overhanging edges. Prepare another two sheets and lay these into the dish at right angles to the first sheets. Repeat this process so that there are eight sheets of filo in the dish.

Gently spread the spinach filling mix over the pastry in the bottom of the dish. Cover the spinach mixture with another two sheets of filo, folded to make them fit. Fold in the overhanging edges of the bottom sheets, and brush the surface with oil or butter.

Bake for 20–25 minutes until golden brown and firm when pressed in the centre. Serve hot, warm or even cold.

VARIATION: Wrap portions of the filling in single (lightly oiled and folded lengthways) sheets of filo, folded or rolled to make individual rectangular or triangular packages.

Country Onion Pie

CHEESY ONION FLAN

This is a simplified version of a tasty flan which Alison has made for years. It makes a popular and economical family meal, and any leftovers go well in school lunches.

FOR 4–6 SERVINGS:

200g bought pastry
1 tablespoon oil
1 large onion, chopped
1 teaspoon (1–2 cloves) minced garlic
1 teaspoon cumin
1/2 teaspoon oreganum
3 large new potatoes, cooked (about 300g)
3 large eggs
1/4 cup milk
1/2 teaspoon salt
3/4 cup grated cheese
paprika

Preheat the oven to 210°C. If you need to pre-cook the potatoes, read the instructions on page 50.

Roll out the pastry thinly on a floured board, then trim to form a 25cm circle. Ease into a 23cm pie plate, fold under the edges and pinch or mark edges with a fork.

Heat the oil in a frying pan, and add the chopped onion and garlic. Cook over moderate heat until onion is transparent and lightly browned. Stir in the cumin and oreganum, then the cubed, cooked potatoes. Mix well and cook until potatoes start to sizzle, then remove from heat.

Break the eggs into a bowl, add the milk and salt. Mix with a fork to blend whites and yolks then add potato mixture from the pan. Stir to mix, then tip filling into the pie crust. Sprinkle with grated cheese and paprika, and bake at 220°C for 20 minutes or until pastry is golden brown and the filling has set.

Serve warm, cold or reheated, alone or with a salad.

PASTRY FOR PIES:

To save time and effort we have used ready-made pastry for our pies. If you prefer filo pastry to other varieties, don't hesitate to substitute it, following the instructions for pies which call for it. Pre-rolled pastry will save you time, especially if you do not have a rolling pin!. Always reseal a filo pack straight after using it, and refrigerate it promptly, so you can use it again later. Look for the newer, lower fat pastries suitable for savoury pies. They tend to make a crisper pie base, especially when rolled thinly.

SIMON'S EASY TOMATO AND FETA TART

In terms of ease and preparation, this is really very similar to a pizza, however, because it uses pastry, we have called it a tart! Delicious and attractive, it makes a great dish to serve to company or for elegant picnics.

FOR 4–6 SERVINGS:

400g block flaky pastry
2 tablespoons tomato paste
1 tablespoon pesto, optional
1 tablespoon water
1/2 teaspoon marjoram
1/2 teaspoon salt
black pepper
250g small ripe tomatoes
1 small or 1/2 medium-sized red onion
1/2 medium-sized yellow or red pepper
1 medium-sized zucchini
1 teaspoon (1–2 cloves) minced garlic, optional
about 8 basil leaves, roughly shredded
2 tablespoons olive oil
100g feta cheese, crumbled
salt and pepper to taste

Preheat the oven to 200°C.

Roll the pastry out until it makes a rectangle (or oval) about 20 x 30cm and 5–7mm thick, transfer this to an oiled or non-stick sprayed baking sheet. Without cutting right through, run a knife around the sheet about 2 cm inside the edge, marking out a smaller rectangle.

Mix together the tomato paste, pesto, water, marjoram, salt and black pepper. Spread this paste evenly over the surface of the smaller rectangle. Cut each of the tomatoes and the onion into 6–8 small wedges. Halve the pepper and zucchini lengthways, then cut it into thin (5mm) ribbons. Combine the tomatoes, onion, zucchini, garlic (if using) and basil leaves in a plastic bag or bowl. Add the olive oil and stir gently until evenly combined and coated with oil.

Spread the prepared vegetables over the paste-covered base, then sprinkle evenly with the crumbled feta. Season with salt and pepper to taste, then bake at 200°C for 20–25 minutes, or until the crust is golden brown and the vegetables begin to brown at the edges.

Serve hot, warm or cold with a green salad or as part of a picnic buffet.

Simon's Easy Tomato and Feta Tart

VERY EASY VEGETARIAN

SWEET TREATS

When we were deciding how to finish this book, we were of two minds. Would we add more main course recipes, or would we pop in a few sweet treats?

In the end, we opted for our 'sweet treats'. We have included the following recipes for several reasons. We wanted anyone who owned this cook book and no other to have a nicely rounded recipe selection. We know these taste really good, and are sure you will enjoy them yourself as well as impressing your friends with them!

We wanted to share these baked recipes because they fit the 'easy' theme of this book, because we feel that there are times when a cup of coffee or tea and a muffin or a slice of Danish is all that is needed for a midday snack, and, importantly, because these recipes have the bonus of including fruit, nuts, seeds and other ingredients that are good for you as well as delicious.

The muffins make great Saturday and Sunday morning treats, will make good additions to weekday lunches, and also freeze well.

The Peach Danish and Filo Apple Strudel make popular desserts for friends, but you'll find that leftovers go down well at any time of day.

Gill's Giant Peanut Butter Cookies and our Jaffa Nut Brownies make good gifts – as long as they don't disappear soon after they are taken from the oven!

Our Easy Fruit and Nut Cake is as much at home up the top of a mountain as it is at a party celebrating a special occasion, and our Apricot Party Cake has been used as a family birthday cake several times, as well as being packed in lunches and (we'll say it quietly) eaten for breakfast!

So, even if you haven't baked before – get cracking, and enjoy the results!

Apricot Party Cake (see page 116)

CRUNCHY LEMON AND POPPYSEED MUFFINS

These muffins are liberally speckled with poppyseeds, which crunch as you bite them. They also have a wonderful, tangy lemon glaze. We find the combination irresistible!

FOR 12 MEDIUM-SIZED MUFFINS:

2 cups self-raising flour
1 cup sugar
½ cup poppyseeds
finely grated rind of 2 lemons
100g butter
2 large eggs
1 cup milk
juice of 2 lemons
¼ cup sugar

Measure the flour, sugar and poppyseeds into a large bowl. Grate in all the coloured rind from the lemons.

Melt the butter in a microwave dish or pot. Add the eggs and the milk and beat with a fork to combine.

Tip the liquid into the dry ingredients and fold together until the flour is dampened. (Do NOT overmix.) Spoon mixture into 12 medium-sized muffin pans which have been lightly buttered or sprayed.

Bake at 200°C for 10–15 minutes until golden brown, and the centres spring back when pressed. Just before muffins are ready, squeeze the lemon juice and mix with the second amount of sugar. (The sugar should not be dissolved.)

As soon as you take them from the oven, brush the lemon and sugar mixture over the tops of the muffins, and the rest over their sides and bottoms. Cool on a rack.

Serve warm or reheated, with coffee or tea, for lunch, or for dessert, with yoghurt or lightly whipped cream.

Crunchy Lemon and Poppyseed Muffins

Blueberry Blue Muffins

BLUEBERRY BLUE MUFFINS

The syrup from the canned blueberries gives these muffins a wonderful blueberry flavour and an unusual 'blue' colour. Being quick and easy as well, they're bound to be popular with cooks and 'consumers'.

FOR 12 MEDIUM-SIZED MUFFINS:

425g can blueberries in syrup
1 large egg
1 cup baking bran
¼ cup canola oil
1½ cups wholemeal flour
½ cup sugar
1 teaspoon baking powder
½ teaspoon baking soda
1 teaspoon cinnamon
¾ teaspoon salt

Open and drain the blueberries, reserving the syrup. Using a fork, mix one cup of the syrup (add a little water if you don't have enough) together with the egg, baking bran and the oil in a small bowl.

Measure the remaining ingredients into a larger bowl and stir well with a fork to combine. Pour in the bran-syrup mixture and stir gently until the flour is just moistened. Avoid overmixing as this toughens the muffins.

Spoon the mixture into 12 non-stick sprayed or lightly oiled muffin pans. Bake at 200°C for 12–15 minutes, until the tops are browned and the muffins spring back when pressed in their centres. Leave to stand in the pans for a couple of minutes, then remove and cool on a wire rack.

Serve warm, cold or reheated, as they are or topped with cottage cheese.

Best Orange Muffins

BEST ORANGE MUFFINS

When you break these muffins open, their wonderful golden colour surprises you; it will brighten the greyest of winter days! If you have a food processor and an orange in the house, try them.

FOR 12 MEDIUM-SIZED MUFFINS:

1 orange (about 200g)
1 cup sugar
1 large egg
½ cup milk or orange juice
100g butter, melted
1½ cups flour
1 teaspoon baking powder
1 teaspoon baking soda
½ cup sultanas or chopped dates
½ cup chopped walnuts, optional

Cut the unpeeled orange into quarters then each quarter into four pieces crossways. Put these pieces and the sugar into a food processor and process with the metal chopping blade until the orange is very finely chopped. Add the egg, milk or extra juice and melted butter, and process until combined.

Sift the dry ingredients into a large mixing bowl, tip the orange mixture into the bowl, sprinkle the sultanas or dates over it, and add the nuts if using them. Then, taking care not to overmix, fold the mixtures together, stopping as soon as the dry ingredients are dampened, but before the mixture is smooth.

Butter (or coat with non-stick spray) 12 medium-sized muffin pans. Spoon the mixture into the prepared pans.

Bake at 200°C for 12–15 minutes, until tops are golden brown and the centres spring back when pressed. Cool in tins for 3 minutes, then lift out carefully.

Serve warm, plain, buttered, or topped with cream cheese or cottage cheese.

MANGO AND MACADAMIA MUFFINS

Mango gives these muffins a delicious fruity flavour, and keeps them wonderfully moist. As an additional bonus, they are relatively low in fat.

FOR 12 MEDIUM-SIZED MUFFINS:

425g can mango slices in light syrup or 1 cup mashed raw mango
1 cup plain unsweetened or fruit-flavoured yoghurt
1 large egg
¼ cup canola oil
1 teaspoon vanilla essence
2 cups self-raising flour
1 cup sugar
½ teaspoon salt
about ½ cup roasted, salted macadamia nuts

Open and drain the mango slices, then transfer the mango to a small bowl and mash roughly with a fork. Add the yoghurt, egg, oil and vanilla essence and mix to combine.

Measure the flour, sugar and salt into a larger bowl. Roughly chop the macadamia nuts, add these to the flour mixture and toss well with a fork. Pour in the liquid ingredients and fold together until the flour is just moistened. Do not overmix as this toughens the muffins.

Spoon the mixture into 12 non-stick sprayed or lightly oiled muffin pans and bake at 200°C for 15–20 minutes until the muffins are golden brown on top and spring back when pressed in their centres.

NOTES: If mango is not available, replace it with canned peaches or crushed pineapple. Macadamias may be omitted or replaced with lightly toasted slivered almonds.

Mango and Macadamia Muffins

PEACH DANISH

Serve this easy cake for dessert or as a coffee cake. For a shorter baking time and a larger amount of topping, choose a larger rather than a smaller pan.

1 or 2 x 425g cans sliced peaches
75g butter, melted
1 large egg
½ cup milk
¼ cup juice from canned peaches
¼ teaspoon almond essence
½ cup sugar
1½ cups self-raising flour
½ cup icing sugar
2–3 teaspoons lemon or peach juice
¼ cup toasted flaked almonds

You can make an adequate cake using one can of peaches, but two cans are nicer, if you have them. Drain the peaches in a sieve, keeping the liquid from the can.

Warm the butter until it melts, in a medium-sized bowl or fairly large pot. Add the egg, milk, ¼ cup of the saved peach juice and the almond essence, and beat with a fork to combine.

Chop the peaches in the sieve roughly, then add about half of them to the liquid mixture with the sugar and flour. Fold everything together until the flour is dampened, taking care not to overmix or break up the fruit. Stop mixing before the mixture is smooth.

Spray or line a cake tin 23cm square (or a roasting pan which is a little bigger), spread the mix over the bottom evenly, then arrange the remaining peaches evenly over the top.

Bake at 190°C for 15–30 minutes (depending on the size of the tin) until the centre of the cake springs back when pressed. Put the hot cake on a rack, or leave in the tin if you can serve wedges straight from it.

Mix the icing by beating the icing sugar with enough peach syrup or lemon juice to make a thick cream. Drizzle this over the warm cake, then sprinkle with the toasted flaked almonds.

NOTES: Toast almonds on an oven tray while the oven is heating up. They should turn light brown in 2–3 minutes.

If you do not want to make icing, sprinkle raw flaked almonds over the uncooked cake, then dust icing sugar over it before serving.

Peach Danish

Filo Apple Strudel

FILO APPLE STRUDEL

Filo pastry makes an impressively good, easy strudel with a light, flaky crust and soft fruity filling. Serve it as a special dessert, for a light lunch, or as a satisfying snack at any time of the day or night!

FOR 6 SERVINGS:

¼ **cup almonds or walnuts**
1 **thick slice bread**
2 **large apples**
¼ **cup sugar**
1 **egg**
¼ **cup sour cream**
1 **teaspoon cinnamon**
½ **cup sultanas or chopped dried apricots**
9 **sheets filo pastry**
about 3 tablespoons melted butter for brushing filo

A food processor mixes the filling easily but is not essential. If you have one, chop the nuts and bread in it, then add the unpeeled apples cut in rough slices. Chop apples to the size of peas. (You may need to do this in two batches.)

Working quickly so that the apples do not brown, add the sugar, egg, sour cream and cinnamon and process briefly. Mix in the sultanas or chopped dried apricots.

Without a processor, stir together the sugar, egg, sour cream and cinnamon in a large bowl, add the bread, broken into pieces and leave it to soften until you can mash it with a fork. Stir in the finely chopped nuts and the sultanas or chopped apricots, then coarsely grate or finely slice the apples and stir everything together.

Open the packet of filo only when the filling is ready. Then, working quickly, take three sheets of filo pastry, and lie them side by side on a dry bench, long sides together, slightly overlapping. Brush with melted butter, using about a teaspoon per sheet. (The whole surface need not be covered). Cover with three more sheets, butter in the same way, then top with the remaining three sheets. (Wrap unused filo airtight, and refrigerate.)

Place prepared filling along the short edge of the large rectangle, then roll up loosely. Brush the whole surface evenly with more oil or melted butter. Cover the ends with foil, so filling stays in place during baking.

Bake on an oven tray lined with baking paper, at 180°C for about 30 minutes, until evenly browned.

Serve warm or reheated, cut in fairly thick slices (with a very sharp knife) with icecream or whipped cream.

Jaffa Nut Brownies

JAFFA NUT BROWNIES

Make these for a treat for yourself, or to give away! Their special, rich texture makes them unique, and very popular. What's more, they are really easy to make. Plain brownies are good, too – for these, just leave out the orange rind and walnuts.

FOR 18 PIECES:

100g butter
75g dark cooking chocolate
2 large eggs
¾ cup sugar
1 teaspoon vanilla essence
rind of 1 orange
½ cup chopped walnuts
½ cup flour

Cube the butter and break the chocolate into pieces. Put both into a microwave bowl and heat for 2 minutes on 50% power, or warm in a medium-sized pot over low heat, until the butter has melted and the chocolate softened. Remove from the heat and stir until smooth and combined.

Add the eggs, sugar, vanilla essence, orange rind and chopped nuts and stir until well mixed. Sift in the flour and fold together, but do not overmix.

Spread the mixture into a 20cm square cake tin with the bottom lined with baking paper and the sides sprayed with non-stick spray.

Bake at 180°C for about 15 minutes or until the centre feels firm when pressed. (Don't worry if the sides rise more than the centre.)

Cool then cut into six pieces lengthways, and three crossways, and store in an airtight container. Dust lightly with sieved icing sugar just before serving.

EASY FRUIT AND NUT CAKE

We consider a slice of this flavourful cake to be an excellent, high energy, nutrient rich, healthy snack, which is compact, easily portable, and long keeping (if it gets the chance). The recipe may be modified to make a richer Christmas or other special occasion cake, too.

FOR A 23CM CAKE:

600g (4 cups) mixed fruit*
½ cup orange juice
150–200g butter
1 cup brown or white sugar
about 1 cup walnuts, pecans or almonds
4 large eggs
1 cup self-raising flour
1 cup wholemeal or plain flour
cherries and almonds, optional

*Buy mixed fruit or use a mixture of sultanas, currants and Californian raisins

Simmer the dried fruit and the orange juice in a large covered pot for about 5 minutes or until all the juice is soaked up by the fruit, stirring now and then.

Take off the heat and stir in the butter (the larger amount makes a richer cake) cut in 1cm cubes, and the sugar. (Pack brown sugar firmly into the cup.) Stir gently until butter melts and sugar is no longer grainy, then stand the pot in cold water to cool its contents, stirring occasionally.

Chop the nuts roughly if they are in large pieces and stir them into the cooling mixture in the pot.

When mixture has cooled to room temperature, add the eggs, beating them in with a fork or other suitable stirrer. When thoroughly mixed, sprinkle the flours over the mixture in the pot and stir everything together.

Pour mixture into a square 23cm tin or two fairly large loaf tins lined with one or more strips of baking paper to cover the bottom and sides. Level top(s), pressing on cherries and almonds for decoration if desired.

Bake cake at 150°C for 60–75 minutes, and loaves for about 45 minutes. When cake is ready, the centre should feel firm and spring back when pressed, and a skewer pushed into the middle (right to the bottom) will come out clean. (A 20cm square cake takes longer.) Sprinkle with a few tablespoons of rum, whisky or brandy if desired. Cool in tin. For best flavour, leave 2 days before cutting.

NOTE: For a richer Christmas cake, use 1kg dried fruit, ¾ cup orange juice and 250g butter instead of the amounts given.

Easy Fruit and Nut Cake

APRICOT PARTY CAKE

This easy-to-make cake contains a can of apricot purée. Made in a fluted cake tin it is truly spectacular, but it can also be cooked in a plain ring tin or loaf tins, with extra mixture in muffin pans. (To check size, fill pans with measured water to see how much they hold.)

FOR 1 LARGE RING CAKE, 12 SERVINGS:

250g butter
1½ cups sugar
445g can apricot pulp
finely grated rind of ½ lemon
2 teaspoons vanilla essence
2 teaspoons ground cardamom, optional
2 tablespoons lemon juice
3 large eggs
2 cups flour
1 cup (140g) ground almonds
2 teaspoons baking powder
1 teaspoon baking soda
½ cup chopped dried apricots
icing sugar

Cube butter and heat in a large pot or microwave bowl just until melted. Take off the heat and mix the cake in the same container. Add the sugar, apricot pulp (2 cups), and the next five ingredients (including the eggs). Beat with a fork or whisk until well combined.

Sieve the flour, ground almonds, baking powder and baking soda into the pot or bowl then tip in any almond left in the sieve. Add the dried apricots then fold everything together. (It is thinner than a normal creamed cake.)

Bake in a large fluted (10 cup capacity) tin, 2 smaller tins, or 1 smaller tin, with extra mixture cooked in muffin pans. Spray tins thoroughly with nonstick spray, then cover this with sieved flour. Bang and turn tin(s) to coat evenly, then tip off excess flour. Do this carefully so the cake will come out cleanly.

Fill tins two-thirds full, to allow room for rising, then bake at 180°C until centre feels firm and a skewer pushed to the bottom comes out clean, for about 45 minutes for the large tin, and less for smaller tins. Tip onto a cake rack 5 minutes after cake is taken from the oven.

Dust with icing sugar before serving. Serve with grapes, straw-berries, etc. and whipped cream, or apricot yoghurt mixed with whipped cream. Eat fresh, refrigerate for several days, or freeze for a couple of months.

GILL'S GIANT PEANUT BUTTER COOKIES

These are a variant of a delicious cookie recipe our friend Gill brought home from New York – like most American cookie recipes, these are slightly chewy rather than crisp when cooked. Gill, a 'chocoholic', swears by the chocolate topping, but this is not an absolute requirement.

FOR ABOUT 12 GIANT COOKIES:

100g butter, softened
¾ cup crunchy peanut butter
1 cup brown sugar
1 egg
1 teaspoon vanilla essence
2 tablespoons golden syrup
1½ cups flour
1 teaspoon baking soda
150g chocolate

Preheat the oven to 180°C. Beat the butter and peanut butter together in a large bowl. Add the sugar, egg, vanilla essence and golden syrup then beat until fluffy (4–5 minutes).

Sift in the flour and baking soda and stir to combine.

Scoop quarter-cup measures of the mixture on to a non-stick sprayed (or baking paper lined lined) oven tray leaving some room for spreading, flatten them out to about 10cm across with the palm of your hand.

Bake for 10–12 minutes until the edges are just beginning to brown, then place two squares of chocolate on top of each biscuit and bake for another 2–3 minutes. Remove from the oven and cool on the tray for 5 minutes, then transfer to a wire rack.

Serve warm with a glass of milk, or cool and store in an airtight container until required.

VARIATION: We like 'giant' cookies, but there is no reason why you can't make twice as many smaller cookies – use one square of chocolate per cookie and reduce cooking time by about 2 minutes.

Gill's Giant Peanut Butter Cookies

IMPORTANT INFORMATION

THE FOLLOWING MEASURES HAVE BEEN USED IN THIS BOOK:

1 teaspoon (tsp) 5ml	$^1/_4$ cup 60ml	1 cup 250ml
1 tablespoon (Tbsp) ..15ml	$^1/_2$ cup.... 125ml	4 cups .... 1 litre

All the cup and spoon measures are level, unless otherwise stated. (Rounded or heaped measures will upset the balance of ingredients.)

Flour is measured spooned (rather than scooped or packed) into measuring cups.

Most butter quantities are given by weight, however small amounts are measured by tablespoon. One tablespoon weighs 15g.

If you are weighing in ounces and pounds, use the following approximations:

1oz 30g	3.5oz l00g	6oz 180g	1lb 500g
2oz 60g	4oz 120g	7oz 220g	2lb .... 1 kg
3oz 90g	5oz 150g	8oz 250g	

If you are measuring in inches use the following approximations:

5mm ...... $^1/_4$ in	10cm...... 4in	18cm...... 7in	25cm...... 10in
1cm........ $^1/_2$ in	12cm...... 5in	20cm...... 8in	30cm...... 12in
2.5cm .... 1 in	15cm...... 6in	23cm...... 9in	

ABBREVIATIONS:

mm .... millimetre	F .... Fahrenheit	kg .... kilogram
cm.......... centimetre	ml .... millilitre	oz .... ounce
in .... inch	l .... litre	lb .... pound
C .... Celcius	g .... gram	

TEMPERATURES AND APPROXIMATE EQUIVALENTS

CELSIUS	FAHRENHEIT	GAS	CELSIUS	FAHRENHEIT	GAS
150°C	300°F	2	200°C	400°F	6
160°C	325°F	3	210°C	425°F	7
170°C	325°F	3	220°C	425°F	7
180°C	350°F	4	230°C	450°F	8
190°C	375°F	5	250°C	500°F	9

Always bring the oven to the required temperature before putting in the food which is to be cooked, unless specified. If you use an oven which does not have a fan, you may find that you need to allow a slightly longer cooking time, or slightly higher temperature.

MICROWAVE COOKING

Microwave cooking times vary, and cannot be given precisely. Microwave instructions have been given for a 650 Watt microwave oven with a turntable.

High	100% power,	about 650 Watts
Medium High	70% power,	about 450 Watts
Medium	50% power,	about 350 Watts
Defrost	30% power,	about 220 Watts

STANDING TIME: Food continues to cook after it is taken out of a microwave oven, e.g. a potato keeps baking for 1–2 minutes.

CAN SIZES:

Can sizes may vary, do not worry if the cans are a little larger or smaller than those specified – it is unlikely to make a difference to your recipe.